Praise for *Honoring Missed Motherhood*

"Through compassionate and open hearted sharing, the authors have created an amazing and insightful presentation of what it means to belong to the 'sisterhood' of missed motherhood. Over the years, women have come to me for spiritual counseling for one reason, only to discover the root of their deep unhappiness was not having the opportunity, due to various circumstances, to care for a child. They would have treasured this book, as will those to whom I will gift it now, as an affirmation of the work we will do together to strengthen their self-image as a person of value and substance. This book will touch the hearts of women, and men, everywhere."

— **REV. SHERRY LADY**, Unity of the
Valley Church, Eugene, Oregon

"This is a long overdue and deeply compassionate book that gives voice to women who may be suffering in silence. Through touching and inspiring stories, Kani and Barbara honor the loss these women have experienced and create a new vision—a world in which the vast numbers of women who miss motherhood can openly recognize and express their loss and be validated as belonging and whole. Their journeys illustrate the cultural shift needed to move the healing out of the closet into shared awareness."

— **LIZA INGRASCI**, CEO/President
Hoffman Institute Foundation

"This book is a must for any woman who does not have children, whether by choice or not! Infertility, career and other life choices are examined within a spiritual context. The author, in a vulnerable and engaging way, guides us through the maze of feelings, societal expectations and breakdowns, into the joy of breakthroughs, healing and triumph of spirit."

—**TAMAR GELLER**, *New York Times* bestselling author of *The Loved Dog* and *30 Days to a Well-Mannered Dog*, founder of Operation Heroes & Hounds and celebrity dog coach

Also by Kani Comstock

Journey into Love, Ten Step to Wholeness
(with Marisa Thame)

Honoring Missed Motherhood

Loss, Choice and Creativity

Kani Comstock

in collaboration with Barbara Comstock

WILLOW PRESS   ASHLAND, OREGON

Copyright © 2013 Kani Comstock

Published by Willow Press
241 Village Park Drive
Ashland Oregon 97520

Cover and Interior Design by Chris Molé Design

ISBN 978-0-9679186-0-0
Library of Congress Control Number: 2013935942

Printed in the United States of America
10 9 8 7 6 5 4 3 2 1

*For all women who have experienced
"missed motherhood," and the people in our
lives who love and support us.*

*If you feel lost, disappointed, hesitant, or weak,
return to yourself, to who you are, here and now
and when you get there, you will discover yourself,
like a lotus flower in full bloom, even in a muddy
pond, beautiful and strong.*

— MASARU EMOTO,
The Secret Life of Water

Contents

Acknowledgments

The inspiration for this book came to me more than a dozen years ago in discussions with my sister, Barbara Comstock, who have been my cherished and wise collaborator on a great variety of projects over the decades. As a result of our many discussions and personal experiences, Barbara and I designed a workshop for women who had "*missed motherhood*" for various reasons and created an outline for a book quite different from this one.

Then life intervened and it was many years before the time was right to create the book. Through those years, however, the idea never left me, even though the form of the book was not clear. Whenever I mentioned the subject of *missed motherhood*, which was fairly frequently, women shared their stories and encouraged me to write this very personal book. Then through surprising and unplanned circumstances, I learned some information that brought my own story full circle. I knew the time had come, and the approach I had to take.

There is a wonderful quotation by Guillaume Apollinaire, which I carry with me whenever I teach, that applies here:

"Come to the edge, life said. They said: We are afraid. Come to the edge, life said. They came. It pushed them... and they flew."

It was attending a workshop a year ago with Alexander Tolken, "Lose Your Mind and Get a Life," which pushed me over the edge. I left the weekend committed to taking six months off from teaching in order to write. I am grateful to Raz and Liza Ingrasci, my employers at the Hoffman Institute, for their wholehearted enthusiasm and support for the project. Their ongoing encouragement made it easy for me to stay on track, even though it took me longer than I thought it would.

I had written the final sections of this book and had begun the third when I realized that this section was building on the work that Barbara and I had done a decade earlier. I asked her to collaborate with me once again. I am grateful that she accepted my invitation and eagerly dug into the subject. As always, her perspective and creativity have enriched the result.

Throughout the writing experience I have felt cheered on by my colleagues, friends and family. In particular, Linda Newlin has been urging me to write this book over many long years; she was there when some of the surprises in my life were revealed to me. Friends and acquaintances have been generous in sharing their stories of *missed motherhood*, some of which are included in this book. In addition, my two brothers—Craig Comstock, a book creation coach, and Bruce Comstock, a balloon pilot, adventurer and manufacturer—have each been writing their own memoirs as I've been writing mine. We have shared many long and varied discussions on writing, which I think have kept each of us going. I give thanks to my preliminary readers, Shoshanah Dubiner, Karen Weiseth and my brothers, who gave me insightful feedback that only made the book better.

Seeing the cover design for the first time was the day this became a book for me. Chris Molé created an image that exceeded my dreams in portraying the message of the book. It has been a joy to work with Chris as she designed the total package. I am extremely grateful. And I thank my editor, Jennifer Strange, who added another perspective and lots of detailed improvements.

Writing this book has been a journey into my past and into some secrets that I have held close, reluctant to share. It was fascinating to watch myself feel uncertain about how much I was willing to reveal to the world. In the end I didn't hold back, but the experience brought alive the unconscious programming that keeps *missed motherhood* hidden.

—KANI COMSTOCK
March 2013

Introduction

The absence of a child or loss of a pregnancy is a void and, frequently, a profound loss experienced as a failure, a lack, a shame, something that needs to be fixed or hidden, even when it is a choice. For the most part, there is no frame, no structure, no rituals, no celebration, no acknowledgment, often even no words. It has no name, no category. The pain, loneliness and awkwardness can be unimaginable until it happens to you.

The birth of a child is universally celebrated. It is the next generation, the continuation of life, a legacy going forward. It has a context. It is about family and belonging and community. It is, in most cases, a joyous event that forever transforms the life of the mother.

One of the first questions often asked when women meet socially is: "Do you have children?" Or: "How many children do you have?" It's as if the presence of children is *the* defining quality of a woman's life. For many women, there is an easy answer—stating the number and genders. But how do you answer these questions if you can't seem to get pregnant, or you suffered a miscarriage, or chose to terminate a pregnancy, or birthed a child and gave it up for adoption, or are waiting for the right circumstances, or don't know if you want children or have decided to live childfree?

When your answer is, "I don't have children," often an awkwardness ensues. Not knowing what to say next, the subject may be abruptly changed. Or, perhaps worse, the probing questions begin: "When are you planning on having them?" "Why not?" Sometimes, unwanted advice is offered.

As we get older, the focus of questions is often on grandchildren. As a childless woman, these questions have been a repeated reminder of what I may be missing, how I don't belong, how I don't fit the norm, how I am out of sync, that there is something wrong with me.

The experience of "not children" has never been named or categorized. It is outside of the expected norm. And so the loss—or, in some cases, gain—is left unacknowledged and not integrated into the woman's life. It assumes a failure to achieve and often creates a sense of shame as well as guilt.

What if "not children" isn't really that unusual? What if the vast majority of women have had, are having, or will have some experience of what I call *"missed motherhood"* in their lifetime?

I have come to recognize five categories of *missed motherhood*—the times in a woman's life when she is not a mother, by chance or by choice:

1. Inability to conceive a child that is wanted

2. End of pregnancy, wanted or not

3. Birthing a child and placing it for adoption

4. Missing the opportunity to conceive, childless by chance

5. Choosing not to have children, to be childfree

Statistics for the categories as I have defined them are hard to come by. Based on available statistics, it appears that as many as 75% of women in America have had or will have an experience of *missed motherhood* at some time in their lives, whether or not they ever have children. This is a stunning percentage! If this is true, the experience of *missed motherhood* appears to be as common an experience as being a mother. It is a part of the norm.

Here's how the statistics break down: In the U.S., *each year* 33% or more of pregnancies (over 2 million) are lost through miscarriage, abortion or stillbirth. By the age of 45 or older, it's estimated that 30% - 45% of all women will have had an abortion and many more will have experienced at least one miscarriage or a stillbirth, 19% are childless and about 10% are infertile.

Millions of women quietly, often secretly, suffer a variation of *missed motherhood* each year. Whether you have experienced *missed motherhood* personally or not, you probably know a woman who has, even though she may have never spoken about it. In sharing with women, and men as well, about writing this book, I have found that almost every one of them brings up how it happened for them in their own life.

Each of us who has experienced *missed motherhood* has our own unique story. As more women delay motherhood, it is increasingly the lack of appropriate circumstances or the inability to conceive. For others, conception takes place and then miscarriage happens. Even when a woman already has children or goes on to birth or adopt another child, the loss caused by miscarriage is real and memorable. Terminating a pregnancy or giving a child up for adoption are choices that incur loss whether or not the woman finds other ways to mother or chooses to be childless. Ambivalence about becoming a mother or the lack of favorable circumstances often end in childlessness. Finally, there are women who choose early and clearly to be childfree. Each of these experiences leaves a woman without a specific child when she might have become a mother.

Personally, the impact of *missed motherhood* has reverberated throughout my life in various and unpredictable ways and from surprisingly different perspectives. It affected my sense of self and my worth, choice of career and friendships, the quality and duration of my relationships, my place in family and society, and my lifestyle. For many years, I felt alone, excluded, not fully feminine.

For a long time I had no idea that the experience of missing motherhood was widespread. Discovering otherwise is what has motivated me to write this book and bring light to the subject so that widespread healing can occur.

Missed motherhood incurs loss whether a pregnancy and child were wanted or not. The extent of the loss and the individual woman's awareness and experience of loss varies. Silence, repression and denial are common strategies for surviving the loss. Ironically, although denial may initially seem to help a woman to cope, when left unacknowledged over time, this loss becomes unfinished business, capturing her creative energy and diminishing her ability to live life fully and in the present.

Recognizing and grieving loss is crucial. Loss attended to—experienced, grieved and healed—can then become integrated into our lives. Owning our entire history is vital to being whole and healthy. But how do we do that? Since *missed motherhood* is held as an aberration, rather than as the common experience it really is, we are left to figure it out for ourselves, mostly alone. Frustratingly, when we do talk about it, we are often admonished to "get over it" as if it were a sore throat. Often, we have no idea how we can heal the pain. So when the sadness does not just go away, or keeps resurfacing, we again can feel inadequate and moved to repress, cover up and ignore the feelings in hopes they will finally go away.

Over my lifetime, I have had lots of opportunity to learn about and reflect on the losses that are incurred by women, and men as well, when motherhood is missed. I experienced it myself, in the lives of my friends and colleagues, and in the lives of hundreds of students I have worked with as a facilitator of an intensive, weeklong, personal development program and as a life coach. Most of these women, including myself, strived to heal the loss by themselves. Some were successful, many were not. Even decades later, mention of the experience can bring tears to their eyes and rip at their hearts.

As I have become aware of the prevalence of the loss and the extent of the continuing sorrow that goes unrecognized, ungrieved and unhealed, I knew change was necessary. It eventually led me, in collaboration with my sister, Barbara Comstock (who has also *missed motherhood* for entirely different reasons), to create from our own healing experiences the opportunities for other women to deal with the impact of their *missed motherhood* loss.

In the last few decades, a variety of books, articles, blogs and websites give voice to the loss incurred in motherhood missed. Generally, each one is limited to one of the five *missed motherhood* categories and primarily focuses on the sadness, silent suffering and isolation caused by the loss. These stories break the silence and create a sense of connection with other women who have had similar experiences. In reading, we can say to ourselves, "Ah, yes, I've felt like that as well. I am not alone." However, most of these sources do not go beyond the single category or discuss the various ways that healing can take place.

Unfortunately, there appears to be an assumption that if another woman has not had the *same* experience of *missed motherhood* that we have had, then she couldn't possibly understand our experience and therefore can't be a resource or a source of support. Even partners often limit sharing their own feelings or curiosity about their partner's feelings out of the belief that their loss is less, that they can't understand what it's like for the woman, or that talking about it with her may inflict more pain. The resulting silence can leave a hole in a woman's life.

As a society, we need to name and include *missed motherhood* as part of the cultural norm. It's necessary to bring it out into the open and offer effective steps for grieving and healing that go beyond what each woman can accomplish on her own, so that each of us can move forward in life with passion and enthusiasm. Women who chose not to have children should be supported in their choice, as well as those who become mothers or those who couldn't. We need a cultural understanding and structure that allows and encourages the healing journey to be shared and supported by community.

This book is a step toward that goal. The first section is the story of my life as it has been impacted by various experiences of *missed motherhood* over the decades, and the ways I struggled and discovered activities and experiences to enable healing so I could move forward to create the joyous life that I love. Other people's names have been changed to provide privacy.

The second section is comprised of the stories of 12 other women, derived from personal interviews, and how they experienced *missed motherhood*. The names have been changed to provide the freedom of anonymity in the telling. Also included in this section is my sister's story, which Barbara wrote herself under her own name. Each woman's story is unique. It has surprised me to discover how many women have not just had one experience of *missed motherhood*, but a combination of several. Each of the women whose stories are included here grappled with the choices and opportunities available to her and, somehow, found a way over the years to create a life that she feels good about. Regrettably, not all women have been so fortunate.

The final section is a collaboration between my sister, Barbara Comstock, and myself. Based on work the two of us have developed over the last decade, it offers ideas and experiences for supporting women who are currently experiencing *missed motherhood*—or have in the past, no matter how long ago—to heal the loss and create lives they can live with passion and excitement. Our hope is that these ideas can be integrated into our culture and communities.

There is an untapped sisterhood of those who have *missed motherhood*. Understanding the shared reality of *missed motherhood*, no matter what the story is, will normalize the experience and evolve a greater culture of understanding and support among all women who have *missed motherhood* and those who love and care for us.

Part One

KANI'S STORY
Challenges and Choices on My Journey

---

*The impact of **missed motherhood** has reverberated throughout my life in various and unpredictable ways and from surprisingly different perspectives. It affected my sense of self and my worth, choice of career and friendships, the quality and duration of my relationships, my place in family and society, and my lifestyle.*

Facing Loss

I had no idea that day how radically my life would change. Up until then I had been delighting in the experience that I could have what I wanted—that my life was turning out even better than I had imagined. My dreams were unfolding, seemingly effortlessly, and I was only 26. I was working on my Ph.D., close to realizing my lifelong passion of being a research scientist. I was married to a man whom I adored, who treasured me, who was also a research scientist. Never before had I experienced the level of support, encouragement and unconditional love he brought into my life. I felt blessed beyond my imagination. Life was an amazing, wonderful adventure.

That day, my husband and I sat together and heard the doctor tell us, "I'm sorry, but you can't ever have children of your own." The finality of those words was stunning, earthshaking, unbelievable. We couldn't really take it in. It was so absolute. It wasn't a total surprise. We had been working on solving the problem. Now we had the conclusion.

Children had always been central to each of our visions of the life we had chosen to create together as a couple, as a family. The plan was to start having children once we could afford childcare, so both of us could continue our work while raising them. It had seemed like the time was right. I was in my mid-twenties and toward the end of my courses, and my husband had a tenured position. We started to try. We researched and discussed possible names—if it was a girl, if it was a boy. We talked about how we would raise our children, what our individual values were, how to discipline. And each month my period arrived like clockwork. Not yet, my body was saying. We were okay with it because we were busy and we had time.

Then, during my annual exam, the doctor found what he thought was an ovarian cyst. Simple surgery, he said—in and out of the hospital in three or four days. Two days after the surgery I regained a consciousness that I remember—but only briefly, until the pain-killing morphine returned me to a stupor again and again. It wasn't until the fifth day that I learned it hadn't been a simple cyst, but massive invasive endometriosis. The cells that should have been limited to the interior of my uterus had escaped and coated every organ in my abdomen. Each month, they had proliferated and shed, placing an inordinate strain on my body to keep up, and had created adhesions that filled my entire abdomen with dense, rigid tissue. My fallopian tubes were sealed closed, my ovaries enveloped.

Suddenly, it was clear why there had been no pregnancy. The doctors said it was the most extreme case they'd ever witnessed or heard of, and they wanted to write about my case for the medical journals. During eight hours of surgery, they had scraped all the organs in my abdomen. The good news was that they had opened the fallopian tubes and said that maybe now I could become pregnant. They suggested we try right away.

First there was recovery from the surgery. Then there were the attempts each month. I remember the attention to my cycle, the planned sex, the tests, the monthly messenger announcing once again: "You are not pregnant." But, at least there was an implied "yet" at the end of the message. And although each of those bloody messages indicated a "loss," the loss was accompanied by a hope that next month things would be different.

This time, however, the doctor's words were clear. There was no hope. The decision was final.

Looking back, many decades later, I see the impact of that decree of infertility was perhaps as profound as when a couple *has* a child. It changed everything forever. I could never go back to the way it was before that event. The dynamic of my life was irrevocably altered.

In the 1960s, infertility was not really discussed and was often referred to with pity. It was a flaw, a failure, a shame. We did not even think of sharing our loss with others. We could not conceive of where to go to find help in dealing with the grief. Back then, therapy seemed limited to the mentally ill, severely neurotic or very wealthy, which did not include us. We were practical, pragmatic people, but we did not know how to deal with this irreparable loss.

From my earliest days, I remember always wanting children. Mothering dolls was training for the only future I could imagine. When I was a teen, I took care of my cousin's six-month-old baby and three-year-old little girl when they came to live with us immediately after a deadly car accident. The crash had killed my cousin's husband and she went into a debilitating depression. Caring for her children was even better than babysitting once a week. It was a prelude, a practicing for my own future life.

As a child I said repeatedly that if I couldn't have children of my own, I would adopt. It puzzles me now why I would say that. I have a vague memory of my father talking about a woman in his office who could not have children of her own and, even as a little girl, I was determined that if that happened to me, I would still have a way to have the family of my dreams.

Here now, following the diagnosis of infertility, was my opportunity to put that childhood pledge into action. Yet suddenly it wasn't that simple. Defeated and depressed that I could not have my own biological children, I also found myself frightened by the challenge of taking on someone else's child. In addition, while my husband desperately wanted children, for some reason not understood by him, they had to be his biologically. He hated his inability to accept adoption as an alternative. He would get angry with himself. We did talk about a surrogate, but never as a serious option. At that time it seemed too outrageous and uncertain.

We talked seemingly endlessly about our limited possibilities for creating a family, but the energy just wasn't there to pursue the available options, which all felt unattractive. The air had been knocked out of us. We had lost our footing and were each sliding down into our own individual pit of darkness. The loss was bigger than we could imagine. It kept growing larger and more encompassing until it encroached on every aspect of our lives.

My husband sunk into his own deep depression that made no sense to him; it overtook his life. He told me he would go to work, put his experiment in motion and stare out the window between readings that needed to be taken. When he returned home at night, he sat and stared as well.

Helpless to stop our own decline, we gallantly attempted to help the other, or at least protect them from any additional suffering. Within ourselves we could find no resolution. We were lost in a trance. There was nowhere to turn for support. We had no solution, no visible options. After a time, we could barely talk to each other about this disaster in our lives and we had no motivation to share our situation with others.

I had lost interest in everything I had been passionate about before. I quit graduate school. I remember my advisor telling me I shouldn't do it, that I was throwing my life away. I was in a daze without any goals.

My husband encouraged me in pursuing any glimmer of interest or curiosity I showed. I tried, but I couldn't find a focus. My passion for life and my joy had dissolved. It was embarrassing to be such a failure. I was in despair and felt that I could never get over this loss. I was derailed, my life turned upside down, my goals erased. In such a brief time, my seemingly perfect life was gone.

Now I was completely alone. I didn't feel I could share my sorrow with anyone else. There was no one who would understand, who would listen and take in what this meant to me and to my life. I didn't want pity. I couldn't stand being told I'd get over it. My mother had been adamantly opposed to my choice of husband, and I dreaded her "I told you so." Life did not seem worth living and I started thinking about death, about ending the pain. I couldn't share this with my husband—he was in his own separate dark hole, suffering and silent. Over many months, I considered various methods of suicide. Luckily I rejected each of them as either unreliable or unacceptable or both. Finally, I came to realize that life on any terms was more attractive to me than death.

Knowing that I chose life, I realized that now I had to find a new path, create a completely different vision for my future. I felt heavily burdened by my husband's pain and depression; he was driven to have his own biological children that I could not have. To me, his situation was even worse than mine because he was trapped by *my* infertility, not his own. I didn't feel that I could live with the pressure of being the cause of his deprivation. So, after many long months of contemplation and desperation, I realized that I could begin to lift the burden of guilt from my shoulders by releasing my husband. I said to him with what I thought was great kindness and generosity, "Please find another wife who can have your children so that you, at least, can have what you want." At first, he was horrified, totally resisting the idea. It took time and a lot of convincing on my part. I was adamant that this was the only way for me as well as for him. Finally, reluctantly, he agreed.

I didn't realize then that I was actually rejecting and abandoning him and sending him away, that my determination to be free of the guilt was actually taking away his freedom to choose. We loved each other deeply. We were intimate friends. I thought we were each sacrificing to make life livable for the other. We would separate and divorce and move on with our individual lives. At times we would joke that, after his future children were grown, we'd reunite and spend our senior years together. This momentarily lessened the grief we felt at leaving each other.

Once we both agreed to the decision, I felt the oppression lift. I felt we were rising out of the deep, dark holes we had each endured for so long. I felt relieved. Once again it appeared we were each on a path with hope for a better future.

We decided that before we would separate, we would do a few things that we had planned, but had not yet managed, to do. We took a long trip to the Pacific Islands and Asia, to the places we had not made it to during our five-month journey a few years earlier, after I had finished my Masters degree and he had completed his post-doctoral research.

During our trip, it felt as if the sun had come out to bless us and we were once again in the light of day. For six weeks we lived each moment and filled each day with exploration, discovery, delicious food, laughter and joy in being together. We bought things for each other that we just couldn't resist. We listened and loved and reveled in the daily adventures that came our way. We had fun. It was, as they say, an altered reality that we wished would never end.

While traveling, we thought we had put the past behind us. We were readying ourselves to go our separate ways while enjoying the relationship we had. I felt clever, like we had triumphed over adversity. It wasn't until much later that I discovered the pain had been buried within.

There had always been an undercurrent before, during and after the travel that we tried to ignore. Once the doctors had determined there was no hope of pregnancy, they had started me on heavy doses of hormones in an attempt to inhibit my menstrual cycle and prevent the buildup of intra-abdominal tissue. But my periods kept coming like clockwork. They upped the dosages. Seemingly unrelated incidents started happening: I would have heart palpitations at times when nothing was going on. Often, I found it hard to focus. Many times I felt faint and, a few times, I did faint.

At work, I frequently experienced what I now know are out-of-body experiences—watching myself from a perch on the ceiling as I attempted to make sense of the scientific articles I was abstracting and editing. I often felt that I was going to die any minute. These symptoms became an almost daily experience. Yet the doctors said there was nothing wrong, that I was "nervous." They gave me tranquilizers, which I never took because I knew that was not the problem.

While we were traveling, the symptoms were muted. It turned out that constantly being with someone I trusted to keep me safe diminished the fear and adrenaline rush, and eating regularly supported a healthier, less-stressed metabolism. Back again at home, the symptoms increased. My husband was often away into the evening doing 18-hour experiments. As soon as I returned from work, I would call him and, between the regular readings he had to take, we would talk all evening to relieve my panic and the fear I felt that I would die that night alone. How ironic that I had now chosen life and felt, almost daily, as if I were going to die.

Finally, by chance, I learned that all my symptoms were from severe hypoglycemia and adrenal exhaustion triggered by the massive hormones that I had been taking. This was great news! Now I knew what was wrong and what needed to be done. I went on a very strict low-carbohydrate, high-protein diet and had injections of adrenal extract to rest my own adrenals. Within a few weeks, I was feeling better. Ready to move on.

Now preparations for separation had to be tackled. I had the further surgery I needed and then, during recovery, taught my husband how to cook a greater variety of dishes. Since he hated to shop, I bought him all the clothes he would need for at least a year. We decided what to do with our "things." We divided our money. We got everything in order. Finally, just before we separated, we told our parents and friends that we were going to get divorced. I had decided I would move away. We said goodbye and off I went. I felt brave.

Everything had changed. Now, I not only would have no child, I also had no husband, no home and no career. I felt that the slate had been wiped clean. Amazingly, I also felt the lightness and spaciousness of being freed from limitation, a release from the heavy burden of shame and guilt and sadness. I had escaped with my life wide open in front of me.

After many heavy months of contemplating ending my life, I had come out of the darkness to view this loss as an amazing opportunity to look at life again with fresh eyes. There was now the possibility of creating a completely different future for myself that I could perhaps even come to love and enjoy. Unknowingly, I kept the grief, the loss, the pain from myself—it was a secret, buried sorrow.

I had unknowingly become a member of an underground sorority of women who experience what I call *missed motherhood.* I had been through the initiation rites with the surgery, the tests, the tears, all those months of not conceiving. But now I was a full-time, permanent member. As I have come to realize, it is a *huge* secret sorority, encompassing a vast number of women in this country and beyond. At that time, I didn't know it. I experienced myself as the exception. I was outside the norm. I didn't belong.

Finding Perspective

If I had known when it first happened to me that *missed motherhood* is a common experience of being a woman, my life could have been quite different. Even now, after more than 40 years and much personal healing and growth, this new understanding brings me an expanded sense of belonging and wholeness as a woman and as a member of society. All of us who have experienced *missed motherhood* should know how widespread it is so that we can all hold ourselves as equal participants in the community of women as a whole.

As discussed in the Introduction, instead of setting a woman outside of the norm, it turns out that *missed motherhood* is just as common and womanly as becoming a mother! This is a radically different perspective that changes the way *missed motherhood* can be perceived as we move forward.

The stories in the next section illustrate that many women have more than one experience of *missed motherhood,* in more than one of the five categories, just as I did. Each occurrence has a personal, and frequently long-lasting, impact for that woman.

Whether chosen or not, all experiences of *missed motherhood* encompass loss. The depth and degree of the loss, the individual woman's awareness and experience of it and her ability to process it, varies and is unique to the individual. Some women feel the loss immediately and frequently this feeling lingers. For others, it surfaces later in life. Some women never allow themselves to recognize it at all. For most of these women, part of the loss they experience is a sense of separation from other women because they feel that they don't meet expectations—their own or others'. There is often a sense of shame, of being not good enough, of failure. Even as I moved on in my life, there was a powerful, often unconscious, undercurrent.

Throughout history, there has been an expectation, unspoken and spoken, that a woman will have at least one child, if not many. It is in her biology. It is in a woman's emotional programming. It is in the culture. The birth of a child forever changes a woman's status. First she was a child, then a woman and, by a certain age, she is expected to have become a mother. In becoming a mother, she creates a family. The age of beginning motherhood is culture-dependent and has changed over the years in this country as women postpone motherhood to establish their careers. But regardless of when, there is a time by which a woman is expected, at least unconsciously, to be a mother and then, eventually, a grandmother.

Nature has designed a woman to have a child. Each month, from our teen years to menopause, we are presented with the bright red reminder of our potential fertility. If a woman is hoping to conceive, the arrival of the monthly menses is a sign of failure. If that flow of blood does not come, then we are left to wonder, "Am I pregnant?" Either a vigil of hope or dread begins—the wait to discover. Now, of course, women can buy pregnancy test kits to deliver the news quickly. How each of us experiences the monthly news is contingent on our plans, our hopes, our vision for our life at that time.

The expectation of mothering is embedded in our language, our social conventions, our hidden and overt responses, in the regular inquiry, "Do you have children?" Historically, children have defined a woman's role and position in society and in the family, and motherhood has been a source of worth, power and belonging. Not bearing children or not giving birth to a child of the proper gender has frequently been reason for rejection or exclusion. Women without children have been pitied and judged as less than whole.

There have always been ways for a woman to consciously step outside this expectation of motherhood; to choose not to be a mother. Often in the past, this included a decision to be celibate or not to be sexual with a man. Failing to reproduce was not necessarily considered *normal* or *natural*, but it was allowed and even accepted, especially if a woman did this to serve her god or humanity.

Women have more choice now than they have ever had before about whether to have a child and when to have a child. With more women choosing and needing to develop full-time careers outside the home, the number of women without children has increased. Some of these women, especially in the U.S., are postponing motherhood into their thirties, forties or even fifties; others are choosing to forego motherhood altogether. Being childless by choice is gaining acceptance, and is often referred to as "childfree."

Through folklore, we learn that over the centuries there have always been ways that have been used to limit conception or terminate unwanted pregnancies. Then late in the 1800s, through the action of an extremely distant relative, Anthony Comstock (who never had any children of his own), all contraception was banned and women had to go underground to limit births. Thankfully, in the last 50 years, birth control options have become more dependable, varied, defined, accessible and acceptable.

Until 1965, when I was already in my twenties, some U.S. states still criminalized the possession and/or distribution of oral contraceptives (the "pill"), even to married couples, until the Supreme Court ruled it a constitutional right. In 1972, they extended the right to include unmarried women. A year later, in 1973, the Supreme Court in *Roe v. Wade* legalized abortion throughout the U.S. as a constitutional right guaranteed to all women. Prior to that time, abortions were performed illegally in "back rooms," frequently by non-medical personnel, which at times left the women scarred and unable to conceive again.

Currently in this country, the availability of some of these options has been severely limited in certain states, and is being actively challenged, limited or denied in others. Having come into adulthood when abortion was illegal and women were frequently damaged irreparably, and contraception was severely limited or unavailable, I find today's threats to a woman's right to choose what's best for her body and life extremely frightening. The ability to decide whether or not to have children and how many children to have is a vital factor in women's economic and personal freedom.

Young women today have been led to believe that it is their choice whether and when they will become mothers. They take it for granted that options exist. With that sense of confidence, they can and do postpone the decision. If a woman conceives, but does not want a child at that point in her life, she might terminate the pregnancy or give birth and give the child up for adoption with a belief that she can always have another child.

When a woman finally chooses to act—to become pregnant—she may find, as many women are finding, that the choice is not necessarily hers. Conception may not occur, or perhaps she conceives and cannot carry the baby to term. Just as she may have benefited by advances in technology in averting pregnancy, she now also has the possibility of being aided in finding a way to conceive or bear a child through advances in fertility treatment, surrogacy or adoption.

With so many choices and options for life, some women are finding that they have postponed motherhood beyond the time it is attractive or possible for them. Perhaps they never found a partner who also wanted to parent before their biological clock ran out. Or, maybe, they are in a committed relationship in which their partner is not interested in having a child. Maybe, as the years went by, they were always ambivalent themselves and never made a clear decision. In the end, it just didn't happen. They missed the chance to choose.

Creating a New Vision

The full impact on women's lives of the loss incurred by *missed motherhood* is often buried and lingers beneath the surface. These losses often feel shameful, to be pitied. We get the message that it's best to keep them hidden, forgotten, wiped out, not discussed. The impact varies for each woman, and for each manner of *missed motherhood*, but it is there for each of us to process, usually alone and often quickly. Unfortunately, we don't necessarily know how to grieve the loss and heal the pain. We don't even know if it is possible. And, if by some chance it is, we don't know where to go to find out.

If we chose to terminate a pregnancy or to not have children, experiencing what we lost by that decision can be interpreted by us (and others) as regret, as if we made the wrong decision, even when we know that it was or is the best choice for us. As a consequence, we may not allow ourselves to grieve—we may even feel that we don't have the right to grieve.

It can seem that only women who had no choice about *missed motherhood*, who are victims of their bodies, deserve the right to weep. And even they are expected to do it privately and quickly.

So, women are left to push it down, cover it over, move on... and moving on is what it feels like we are supposed to do. Replace the lost child with another one and it will be like the loss never happened. And it can seem as if it does. But the loss unprocessed remains a weight, often suppressed and unrecognized, a weight that saps our energy and can bind up our creativity and diminish our ability to live our lives fully.

As I described earlier, my clearly defined loss sent me spiraling down into darkness. The gates of my imagined future had been slammed in my face. It was so extreme that I could not slip into denial. I had to face the loss full-on and experience the grief. I couldn't sidestep it. The energy went out of my body and I was a sleepwalker through days that brought no joy. I lost interest in everything.

I have always been persistent and responsible and it was no different at that time. I went through the motions of life. I did my assignments at work. I cooked and cleaned and stared out the windows. I didn't like who I had become. I tried to pursue anything that provided a spark of interest in me. I couldn't imagine going on this way. Everything that I had loved and cherished and felt so blessed by until that time had unbelievably lost its meaning.

The clear verdict from the doctor on my infertility was brutal and traumatic to hear. That it was absolute was also, in the end, supportive of my experiencing the loss deeply, so that I could then move forward with a clean slate so to speak, and create a different vision for my life that I could enter into enthusiastically.

In the 1960s, there were very limited choices for a woman in my condition. The possibility of *in vitro fertilization (IVF)* was far in the future. In fact, the choices I knew of were adoption and the newly-discussed and rarely used possibility of surrogacy. Once they were ruled out by my husband and me as unacceptable, there was only childlessness.

Another possibility that is offered to childless women is to involve themselves in the lives of their friends' or siblings' children. Only one of my three siblings had a child. They were keenly aware of my infertility and subsequent divorce and, while I was living in Japan, it was decided by them that I would become my niece's godmother. I wasn't there, or even consulted. It was announced. Since they lived far away through all of the years my godchild was growing up, I rarely had a chance to spend time with her. But I have enjoyed the times we've had.

As a result of the severely limited choices at the time when infertility happened to me, I didn't spend years in limbo attempting to bring a child into my life through one of the many options currently available. I have younger friends now who have spent a decade or more doing this, enduring loss after loss. Some eventually succeeded, others never did.

The power of visualization has been well documented now, but 40 years ago I had never heard it spoken about. As we hold a vision of what we want to create, we are benefitting from the power of that vision in bringing it forth into reality. I had done a great job of actualizing my original vision for my life, until I hit the final piece: children. As long as I held the vision that I needed children (and a husband) to be happy and fulfilled, I was a dismal failure. Thankfully, I realized that I could end up living my entire life believing that I had missed out on what truly mattered to me. I couldn't bear that.

In desperation, I recognized that as long as I held onto my old vision, I was a victim of life, a loser—that childlessness had been done to me and I had no choice. I would have to settle for second best. I wasn't willing to do that. There was no energy in that option. It was debilitating and exhausting.

I realize, looking back, that I benefited from my father's repeated advice and encouragement to create a life I loved. I definitely was *not* loving being a loser. I knew with great clarity that my energy rose when I was interested in something and excited by the discovery involved in pursuing those interests. I loved that feeling of being fully present, excited, lost to time and totally involved. I wanted to feel that way again.

When loss happens, it is easy to feel that it was done to us. We can feel a victim and ask, *Why me?* We can surrender to thinking, *My life is ruined, I'll never get over this.* It is so easy to get stuck. I did. I was horribly stuck in the loss that happened to me. I had no solution. I was ashamed of myself. I was ashamed of the inadequacy of my body. I was frustrated by my inability to cope, to rise above, to find a solution. I felt there was no solution. My life was over.

As I have learned repeatedly over the years, no matter what happens, we always have choice. We may not like the choices, but choices exist. Loss and choice, choice and loss, are inevitably linked. When we experience a loss—no matter how large or small—there is always choice about how we will deal with the loss and move forward. The pain of the loss can blind us to this. A big loss, like the inability to conceive, can be so painful that we cannot seem to find a way out.

So my task was to open my mind, to expand beyond the self-imposed limits of the past and imagine what could enliven and fulfill my life now. I had to let go of the former dream, surrender to what was and consider the opportunities that were actually available to me if I crossed off motherhood.

We make choices all the time, big and small: which job to take, what house to buy, who to marry, where to go on vacation, which car to buy. Every time we make a choice, we lose the other options that were possible or considered. If we are really excited about the option we have chosen, we may not feel the loss for long, or notice it at all, but it is there. When the choice is not ours to make, when it happens *to* us or is the result of another person's action, the loss can sting and linger as a sign or a rebuke that we do not have the control.

Knowing that choice involves loss can make us wary of choosing, because we know we have to let the other options go. Many times this knowledge holds us back from making any decision, especially if there is no outward deadline and the thing or experience we are giving up is precious to us. We can waste valuable time. Many years or even decades can go by. Not choosing also creates loss. We can end up, years later, regretting the time lost in uncertainty or indecision.

I think it is human nature to want to believe that we can control our lives and make happen whatever we desire. In each of our lives, there are many things we can and do control. Eventually, we come to realize that absolute control is not part of being human. But we can always control the choices we make, the action we take, what we choose to do with circumstances that come our way. In recent years, there have been so many horrific natural disasters. Tornadoes have destroyed huge swaths of towns and left only devastation in their paths. Hurricanes and floods, earthquakes and tsunamis have wiped out vast areas. The economy imploded, many lost their jobs, their houses, their hope. I lost the dream of having my own child.

In time, it came to me that I needed to release my long-held dream of family. I had to say goodbye to that old, beloved, delicious dream in order to discover a future worth living. The darkness and depression that I experienced as a result of the verdict was so awful that, if I was to live, I realized I had to create a completely different life. It couldn't just be a little modification so that I would always rub up against the loss and the hurt. I didn't want to settle for humdrum. It had to be a life that was exciting to me, one that I couldn't wait to begin. By deciding that it had to be a life that would not have been possible if I had had children, I opened a vast field of opportunity that had been out of my imagination previously.

First, I moved to the San Francisco Bay area. It was a time before the rules had changed, when employers could ask you everything about your life, and they did. My education and marital status worked against starting fresh, so I learned to withhold information just to get a job to pay the rent. Within a few months, I knew I was in a holding pattern that brought little satisfaction and was going nowhere. I really wanted to take a giant leap into another reality. I wanted to move to Japan. The country and its culture had fascinated me since childhood and I had spent time there during my travels. I stayed in California and worked long enough to get a work visa and a job teaching English as a Second Language (ESL) in Tokyo. I received my divorce decree the day before I left the United States.

I abandoned everything and everyone I knew. I stepped out into the unknown with delight. Free of the past restrictions and disappointments,

I was now eager to move forward. Teaching English in Japan was a far cry from basic scientific research and I was starting from scratch. It kept my mind busy. And, as I taught the students, I learned more and more about the culture and the customs. I lived Japanese-style, went to the public bath, slept on *tatami*. I studied the language. Life was so new and different. I had a lot to learn just to do my job. The wonderful juiciness of curiosity and exploration and discovery stimulated my creativity.

I took on the challenge of this new life and new work. Within a year of my arrival, and in collaboration with other teachers, I had come up with ideas for reframing the curriculum to be more effective. I convinced the president of the school to give it a try. Suddenly, I was the curriculum director—the first non-Japanese ever in that position! I was having fun. I reorganized the office so that the women there had more responsibility and room to use their creativity. I designed a program for students to travel to the U.S. and stay in American homes. I ended up as the first non-Japanese director of the school. I couldn't have done this if I'd had a family; it would have been inconceivable.

I created a lively community of friends and colleagues—Japanese nationals and expatriate Canadians and Americans (none of whom had kids or even spouses)—and I fit in. I had found a place where I could belong. I was an adventurer. No one ever asked me if I had children or even a husband. I was taken at face value. My life was fascinating, creative, carefree and joyful and I loved it. As an outsider, I could create and live by my own rules. For the first time in my life, I had a few affairs. One advantage was that I didn't have to worry about getting pregnant!

My former husband, Hiro, who had been born and raised in Japan, visited a number of times while I was there. We would meet for a meal and usually also visit his father and sister in Yokohama. Since our divorce, his family had repeatedly made it clear that I was always welcome in their home. Hiro was not yet married, still had no children. His father and sister teased us about getting back together. They didn't care about children, but it was not even a possibility for me. I couldn't imagine going backwards.

By the second year, I had a steady partner who was charming, creative, committed, attentive, sexy, seven years younger and very lovable. (A blonde Caucasian woman in Japan has a lot of opportunity for choice and I have always been attracted to Asian men.) Life was one new experience after another. I felt rejuvenated, fully alive. I loved my partner and felt loved by him and supported in my lifestyle. I was delighted with my choices and happy with my life as a single woman without children. I had miraculously found my way out of the depth of despair and into joy. I felt lucky.

After several years in Japan, the pain came, physical pain in my side, in my belly. I had all sorts of tests. There was no explanation other than endometriosis. It had returned with a vengeance. Slowly, and only occasionally, I began to use painkillers when the pain was unbearable. It helped. They had told me after my earlier surgery that I would eventually have so much pain that I would need to have a hysterectomy, by the time I was 40, they predicted. Gradually, some level of pain was there almost constantly; it was the background of my life. Eventually, I was frequently taking Darvon to keep it dull.

For a combination of reasons, after living and working three years in Tokyo, I decided it was time to leave my life in Japan—I'd already stayed longer than I'd planned—and return to the U.S. My partner and I had discussed for some time that he was going to follow me so he could fulfill his dreams of study and work in aviation. Once again, I packed up my things, said goodbye to all my friends, colleagues and work, and moved toward an uncertain future. I had no idea what I would do next. Not knowing had become not only acceptable, but exciting.

So Many Choices

There had been a remarkable change in the U.S. while I was gone. The feminist movement, which began before I left for Japan, had expanded and was impacting the culture in wonderful ways. I remember that, while living in Japan in 1972, a fellow teacher received one of the first editions of *Ms.* magazine, which we all read with amazement. Laws were changing and women were gaining more equal rights.

Earlier, when I was in graduate school, a professor I had wanted to work with had refused to be my advisor. He told me that advising female graduate students was a waste of time because they would get married and have children and drop out of research. That attitude was acceptable then. As I learned when I was trying to get a job in San Francisco in 1970, employers could inquire about personal information and assumed that I would return to my husband, as well as go back to science research. That kind of treatment was legal then. But it wasn't anymore!

While it had been quite easy in Japan to get a job that was completely outside my field of study, back in the U.S. I was floundering. I was trying to figure out, first of all, what I wanted to do and, then how to get a job doing it. All my education was in science, but I knew I didn't want to go back. Now I had experience in teaching English as a Second Language, studying Japanese language, learning about that culture and managing an organization. But I didn't know if and how I wanted to use any of that knowledge. I knew I wanted to move forward. From the challenges I had already faced, and the solutions that had worked for me, I knew that I needed to be excited about the work I did. So I started exploring.

Very quickly I lucked upon a workshop led by Ranny Riley and her fairly new organization, "Career Design," which taught steps for discovering and creating a position that would utilize my unique set of skills and interests. While I was using those steps to explore my possibilities, it also turned out that my skills were useful in developing her company and it was fun leading some of those workshops. It was only part-time, but it was a foothold back in my native land.

The pain in my body was a continuing challenge. I read an article that said the Darvon I was taking to dull the pain could be dangerous. I quit taking it. Once again, my life was being squeezed by the limits of my body. I remember driving on the freeway in the midst of a minor panic attack exacerbated by the adrenal rush of my hypoglycemia, fighting for control of myself and my life. I pulled over to the shoulder to calm down, to wait until my rapidly beating heart slowed. Sitting there watching the cars rush by, I remember deciding that I was not going to allow my body to control me. I was going to learn to maximize my physical well-being. I was not going to have a hysterectomy. (I never have.) Without realizing what I was doing, I visualized my life without the pain. Over years, the pain subsided, although occasionally it reappeared. I went on with my life.

Within the year, I found myself creating a center for teaching English as a Second Language at a small college in the area. This was exciting and challenging. The mid-70s was the beginning of the great influx of foreign students to the U.S., especially from the newly oil-rich countries. There were very few colleges teaching ESL courses. There were no degrees for teaching ESL yet. So I hired teachers returning from the Peace Corps and others, like myself, who had taught ESL overseas. We got to start from scratch, drawing upon what I had learned in Japan and what my faculty had learned in the countries where they had lived and taught. We created a structure that we could apply in a college setting with students coming from many different countries. Every six weeks, we would get a new group of students whom we tested and placed in one of six different levels in five subjects—that's 30 courses. Once again, I had created a childless environment. Neither the ESL faculty nor the students were married or had children. I fit right in.

Periodically, my ex-husband would appear—still unmarried, still no children of his own. It was always fun to see him, catch up on his adventures. But after a few more years (more than five had passed since our divorce) with no romances apparent in his life, I was angry at him. Finally, at the end of a visit, I accused him of not keeping his part of the bargain. We had gotten divorced so he could have the children of his own that were so necessary for him. He had to get busy and reproduce. That was the last time I see or hear from him for over 15 years.

Time went by, and each year I was able to take on new projects that challenged my creativity. The ESL center was thriving. We had as many as 300 students at a time. As they moved into the college degree programs, the student body became more and more international. I got to work on internationalizing the curriculum, especially the courses around business, finance and management. The impact of global crises was felt in the college and in the classroom, the biggest of which was the run-up to the Iranian revolution, the Iran hostage crisis and subsequent events.

There came a time when I was feeling tired, endlessly, no matter how well I ate or slept. I couldn't figure out what was going on, but I thought maybe it was somehow connected to my prior hypoglycemia. I went to my endocrinologist. After checking out various possibilities, what we found was that I was pregnant! I was in shock, stunned!

Twelve years earlier, I had been told this could never happen for me. My medical records clearly showed that pregnancy was an impossibility. My life had been torn apart. I had surrendered my marriage and had lost all interest in my previously beloved scientific research. I had given up my dream and created a different life, which I was currently enjoying immensely. And now, unbidden, unbelievably, unwelcome, I was with child. It was embarrassing and felt cruel. After all the grieving and healing and growing I had done to make my life livable, I could no longer conceive of having a child. It was unthinkable. I had destroyed the life that had a place for one and created a different reality. It felt like a cosmic joke. I could not go back to my previous life or my previous dream.

The relationship from which this fetus was conceived was tenuous and uncommitted. I had created a life in which motherhood did not fit, where *not* having children was an advantage. I was not prepared to be a single mother—I had never been interested in that. It was completely out of the question. I knew with total clarity that I would have an abortion, which was now thankfully legal and supported by the father. This pregnancy was so medically unlikely that before the abortion procedure, the doctor asked me to have a sonogram. (I realized much later that there was some possibility of it being an ectopic pregnancy.) The technician, not knowing of my decision to abort, took a photograph of the fetus, which I have to this day. I held the pregnancy as a message that I was not flawed. I was whole.

I have never regretted my decision. It was right for me. In this I had a clear and available choice. I was not forced by circumstances to radically change my life as I had more than a decade earlier. But it has also been my secret, shared with only a very few. My brother wholeheartedly supported me and took me to the procedure. My sister, far off in Nepal, was on my side. My mother and father never knew, nor did most of my friends or my ex-husband. It has been a hidden fact of life that did not fit my storyline.

I was raised in a time when contraception was limited (this was before the pill) and abortion was illegal. I knew of girls who disappeared from school, much later to return. I knew stories of back alley abortions where young women were mangled by non-medical personnel. Just a few weeks ago, in talking about this book, a friend shared with me about her own illegal abortion as a teenager. When I asked if she had ever told her grown daughter about it, she said no, but that she had warned her about getting pregnant. It reminded me once again that so much about *missed motherhood* is still hidden, secret, underground—even to this day. "Normal" is held as having children. Not having children has been viewed as flawed, questionable or selfish, although now it is becoming more acceptable.

Certainly when I was a child, it was considered pitiful when a woman—and it was always about the woman—couldn't conceive. It was considered strange, not natural, when a woman didn't want children, and shameful if she couldn't have them. It was understandable that a husband was unhappy if his wife did not produce a child.

Decades later, when contact was re-established, I was to learn that Hiro, my former husband, finally had his first child just a few years before my own pregnancy. How ironic it was that our lives played out that way. If I had not healed the loss and created a full life, that news could have been devastating to me. When I learned about his children, I was actually delighted for him.

Over and over, events develop that have demonstrated to me that we cannot know what the future will bring forth. Life is a continuing adventure with many small and large choices available along the way. We need to be willing to live in the present and walk bravely into the mystery that unfolds before us, open to perceiving, creating and recognizing arising opportunities that are often beyond our previous conception.

Later the same year, I went to Nepal to visit my sister and brother-in-law and got amoebic dysentery, a mysterious lump in my belly the size of a grapefruit and severe pain. The embassy doctor said I needed intravenous antibiotics, which were not safe to receive in Nepal. It appeared I had an abdominal infection that could rupture and cause peritonitis and death. I went from the doctor directly to the Kathmandu airport. I flew via Bangkok to San Francisco and then went straight into Stanford Hospital for ten days of maximum-dose, intravenous antibiotics. It helped, but didn't seem to resolve the problem. They hadn't yet figured how to do noninvasive surgery through the belly button to see inside, so, a few weeks later, I had abdominal surgery with a huge incision just like the first surgery. They found that, during the infection, my intestine had wrapped itself around my ovary and had adhered along with my fallopian tube. They removed the ovary and fallopian tube and found there was no remaining infection and, miraculously, no sign of any endometriosis or scarring. Somehow, my body had healed itself!

In the next few years I re-entered the relationship with my former partner from Japan, who wanted to marry me and proposed regularly, at some periods almost every day. I still would not, could not, take such commitment seriously. My fear that not having a child would eventually destroy the relationship came floating up to haunt me. Now, having been pregnant once, I thought that a child was possible. We talked about it. Previously, he had been totally accepting of my inability to conceive and now he was accepting of having a child. It did not seem his issue. He loved children. They did not have to be his own. We never used birth control and I never became pregnant again, which was fine with me. Some years after the abortion, I learned through another medical procedure that my uterus was malformed and might never have even supported a pregnancy.

Fertility issues have been the backdrop of most of my adult life. At first it was simple—I couldn't have children and I couldn't expect to talk about it with anyone. When people would ask if I had children, I replied, "No, I *can't* have children." This indicated that I wanted them, that I had tried but had been unsuccessful. That would often abruptly end the conversation; I never knew why. I thought it might be because they didn't know what to say, that they didn't know if they'd stepped into a swamp and soon would be under water. Others would pursue the issue, asking about adoption or a surrogate, as if children were a requirement of a full life.

It became more complicated after I got pregnant and had the abortion. I was so imbued with the saga of my childlessness that I now did not know what to say. Once again, it was embarrassing. I felt that nature had made a fool of me and I had participated in the joke. So I kept saying the same thing because, for me, that really was the explanation of why I had no children. First, I was told I *couldn't* have children. Then, unbelievably, it seemed that I could. The possibility was now there, only this time I was not at all invested in getting pregnant—and I didn't.

What would I say now? How could I explain? It was a long story. I could have just said no, which could lead to more questions. So I would say, "Not being able to have children was the great trauma in my life," because that, to me, is the truth about my childless state. If I had gotten pregnant when I was married, I would have a child. But being judged as infertile had dramatically diverted the course of my life and I had no interest now in reversing the flow.

Ever since the infertility decree in my twenties and the subsequent divorce, I can see, in hindsight, that I had avoided commitment in relationship as an unconscious means to shield myself from hurt, from abandonment, from re-experiencing my perceived inadequacy. Now I was in my forties and my partner wanted more. He said he didn't care about having children. I, however, had no interest in commitment or desire to get married. I did not want to lose again. I could not risk the pain. By the time I worked through that issue for myself, 14 years after the relationship initially began, my partner had lost interest.

I do not belong in any single category of *missed motherhood*. I was told I could not conceive; it had been medically decreed that I could never become pregnant and I dramatically adjusted my life. I created a new vision of a life without children that was satisfying and fulfilling, even though, unconsciously and deep-down, I felt less than whole. Then beyond all imagining, I conceived under circumstances that held no joy for me. I did not want to adjust again. I did not have the interest or flexibility to even consider single parenthood.

Now the story was really too complicated to share, so I covered up, pushed it aside, never spoke of it. Then there was the small possibility that I could conceive in a relationship that would welcome a child and it did not happen. I couldn't openly move over into the category of choosing not to have children—that would deny the trauma that determined much of my life path. So I stayed in hiding, without a satisfactory reply when asked. Finally, time ran out on possibilities. I have no children of my own, no adopted child or stepchild, and I have no grandchildren. I really like the life I have created and am happily childfree.

Opening to Joy

Work was my salvation. I loved it. I loved the opportunity to use my creativity to bring forth what did not exist before. It was not a baby or a family, but it was totally involving and satisfying and fulfilling and ultimately fun. It was also under my control. I got myself into work situations where I could choose my projects, push up the deadlines to get things done faster, work with colleagues who enjoyed collaboration and celebrate the accomplishments. I even found it satisfying to gather the troops to untangle the messes when things didn't happen as projected. I loved the challenge and the intensity and even the long hours. When I had accomplished all that intrigued me in one organization, and had set it up to continue after I was gone, I moved on to another that offered even more interesting challenges.

In my mid-forties, having accomplished all I'd set out to do and more in my executive position, and having hit the limit of possibilities in my current company, I was preparing to resign. I would find another, even more, challenging professional adventure. Luckily, in thinking about my next move, I came to realize that I'd become a workaholic—addicted to the high that work provided to me. I also realized that I was in a relationship with another workaholic, so our habits supported each other. Our life was compartmentalized. We did nothing but work from Monday to Friday and then spend the weekend together recovering so we'd be ready for the next week.

When I did quit, instead of finding another job right away, I decided I would take three months off to learn how to have non-work fun—a task at which I was a total failure. I used all those months getting the many little things in my personal life taken care of that I'd not had time for previously. And when that was done, I was so bored that I just wanted my briefcase back, a new challenge and those exhilarating 80-hour workweeks. Fortunately, my new awareness of my addiction to work made it possible for me to refuse to just step back into that.

It's said that "when the student is ready, the teacher will come," and that's what happened for me. As I was despairing about how to find any way to really change, the possibility of some amazing personal growth work appeared on my path. I jumped into it, which was not like me at all. My past scientific training had fine-tuned my analytical approach to decisions: I would carefully study a situation from all sides and make a thorough evaluation before coming to any conclusion. Not this time. I was so frustrated in attempting to change—and so ready to change— that I was willing to jump in with both feet. Well, actually, I first read a book describing the work, not once, but twice in only 24 hours. Both times it touched something deep down within and I found myself at moments in tears. So I signed up for this eight-day residential course called the Hoffman Process. Soon I was doing the extensive written pre-work, which brought up more unrecognized emotions that were lurking within and made it clear that I had a lot to work on.

Those eight days were amazing. It was a mind-blowing process of self-discovery, not just from intellectual analysis, but derived from cathartic experiences that revealed emotions and beliefs that were previously submerged within. The process enabled change to happen. Each day built on the experiences and discoveries of the days before. I came to understand the specific ways that my childhood had impacted my adult life and created drives and limitations that were beyond my conscious control. I also learned and experienced how to change those limiting beliefs and open myself to living in the present from more creative alternatives. The learning and change that happened brought me what I didn't even know I was looking for, more than I knew was possible. It opened me to the abundance of choices available to me, expanding the dimensions of my life. I found an "ease" I had never known before. It has forever changed my life.

It was stunning to begin to grasp how profoundly the experiences of our early years, especially birth through puberty, impact our brains, unconsciously as well as consciously. Those experiences created patterns for me, mostly without my consent (and many times inaccurately) about how to be and what I needed to do to belong and to be loved, worthy, safe and successful. The force of these beliefs was powerful and often previously unquestionable.

In the Hoffman Process, I finally came to understand the power of the unconscious forces that had made it impossible for my ex-husband to release the need to have his own biological children. I know he dearly wanted to release this drive. He loved me deeply and didn't want the marriage to end. It had pained him greatly—I think it did for the rest of his life—that the drive for his own children felt so primal and so strong that he could not change or overcome it, no matter how strenuously he worked on it with his powerful intellect. With the new understanding I gained, I found even more forgiveness and compassion for him.

Doing the Hoffman Process opened another huge chapter in my life, one that eventually evolved into an experience of parenting in a manner previously inconceivable.

Soon after I completed the Process, the founder, Bob Hoffman, asked me to become the executive director. Building on my background with international organizational development, I was able to help him bring the Process to other countries and organize it for growth. I did it out of gratitude for the impact the Process had had in my life and the desire to enable others to experience these changes in their lives. Within a few years, I also trained to become a Hoffman Process Teacher so I could be a better director. I found that I loved the teaching and working with students and helping them to discover and untangle the impact of their childhood years. In an unimaginable way, it enabled me to be involved in parenting—briefly, quickly and deeply—for thousands of people.

Back then, the kind of work we were doing in the Process was not supported by all the research that is now available. It was on the fringe for many people. While Bob Hoffman had written a book more than 15 years earlier, since then the Process had been refined and restructured into an even more powerful form. What we wanted was for someone to write a new book. Over time, we discussed who that could be. We had various successful authors as students who loved the work. But nothing had clicked. The thought started floating in my mind: *Kani, you need to write the book.* While I had done a fair amount of scientific writing and editing, I repeatedly brushed off the thought as ridiculous. I was too busy and not really interested in doing it myself. Finally, when once again the thought arrived, I grabbed onto it and said, *Okay, I'll do it!*

If I was going to write a book, I wanted it to be fun and collaborative. By this time I had become great friends with a Brazilian colleague, Marisa Thame, who was the director of the Brazil center for the Hoffman Process in Sao Paulo. Whenever we would get together in one country or another, we'd spend hours each day talking about the Process: how to develop our individual institutes, expand the Process, train teachers. We both loved ideas and we loved creating. So, on the next trip to Brazil, I suggested we write a book together. Marisa, ever practical, asked, "I can barely speak English, how can we write a book?" I suggested that we discuss our ideas and I would write and then we would edit it together. We could have the finished product translated into Portuguese so each of us would have a book on the Process in our country. This is what we did, chapter-by-chapter. Marisa, like me, was unmarried and childless. Once the book was complete, she always referred to it as "our child"—the product of our joint creativity. I liked that. The book is entitled, in English: *Journey into Love, Ten Steps to Wholeness*, and is also published in Portuguese and Spanish.

Over the years, the combination of being both a Hoffman Teacher and Life Coach became my passion. After a decade as director, I transitioned out of that role and into full-time teaching, coaching and project development. For over 20 years, I have had the honor of guiding and supporting thousands of people in the adventure of changing their lives—just as I'd been able to change mine—and discovering and becoming more authentically themselves.

It was as a Process Teacher and coach that I witnessed and regularly worked with the repressed pain of unprocessed loss, including the loss incurred in miscarriage, abortion, giving a child in adoption and infertility. A standard question in the pre-work revealed that more than 50% of students had one or more experiences of miscarriage or abortion, which I now call *missed motherhood*, in their history. Frequently, when asked about it, tears flowed, even if it had happened decades earlier—and this was often true for men as well as women. Many times they were surprised that the pain and sorrow were still there.

One of the delights of teaching the Hoffman Process is the amazing students from all different backgrounds and fields of endeavor who show up out of a desire to be more fully alive, authentic and whole. Many of them are authors, workshop leaders and healers who have been involved for a long time in personal growth and spiritual healing and development. They come to the Process to continue their own personal development. Sometimes, at a time after they have completed and integrated their Process experience, I have the opportunity to benefit personally from their work and expertise.

One of these healers is Elizabeth Lawrence of the LuMarian Center (*lumarian.net*). In a session with Elizabeth, as she was working on opening my chakras, she asked if I had ever had an abortion. This was my secret. Only a few people knew about it, so I was surprised by the question. I hesitated answering for just a moment, realizing that I had to be truthful if I wanted to benefit from her work. "Yes," I said. "When I was younger, I had been told I was infertile, could never conceive, had undergone surgery and then, at close to 40 years old, I became pregnant. The child's father knew of it and was supportive of my decision to abort. I have never regretted the decision. The solution had been clear to me." Elizabeth then asked me to call forth the soul of that child and say whatever needed to be said. Without thought, from my heart, I thanked the soul of that little being for coming to me for that brief time to bring some healing to me that I am whole, I am a woman. Then she asked me to receive the soul's message. What I heard was: "You are whole and you have always been whole." This was a brief but powerful few minutes in a much longer session. At the end of the session, my heart and arms felt tingly, like when a body part has been asleep and feeling begins to return.

My sister, who has herself experienced *missed motherhood*, is also a Hoffman Process Teacher. After sharing with her how powerful it had been to speak with the soul of the child, we decided to introduce an opportunity for students to do something like this in the Process we were teaching. Initially, we just did it with our own students and found it so meaningful for them that it became a regular part of the Process. At a particular time, the teacher goes to the appropriate students individually, with flowers in hand, and notes that they had indicated in the pre-work that they had previously had an abortion and/or miscarriage. Often, this is a point when tears well up in the eyes of the student, even decades after the event. We suggest to them: "If you choose to do so, you can take a flower for each of these little beings and find a beautiful spot in nature and place a flower there. Then speak out loud whatever you want to say to that little being. Take your time. Then, perhaps even more importantly, you might choose to ask for and listen to a message that little being has for you."

Many students are profoundly impacted by the opportunity both to speak and to hear from that little being who had been in their life and was no more. Many students have had more than one experience of *missed motherhood*. Some had a whole bouquet of flowers. Often, they had no idea there was so much feeling repressed. We started doing this with just the women at first. Then we also included the men. Many men, as well as women, remarked that it was one of the most powerful experiences of the week.

In addition to past miscarriages and abortions, there are women who come to the Process challenged by the inability to conceive, possible infertility and the question about whether they want to bring a child into their world. The ability to show them how to discover the unconscious belief systems that cloud or drive those issues make it possible to support them in finding healing and resolution as they move forward.

Recent brain research is confirming that so much of what we want in life, what we think we need to feel worthy and whole, is a result of patterns unconsciously programmed into our brains when we are children. Patterns are beliefs that we took on unconsciously or consciously in response to our experiences from birth through childhood. Our brains hold these beliefs as truths—whether they are or not—about the way life is, the way the world is, what we can expect, what we must do to be loved, safe, successful, worthy and to belong. These patterns drive us, limit us and define the boundaries of what life can be.

This was true for me. My vision from childhood was becoming a research scientist, getting married to a wonderful, loving man and having children—a loving, happy family. I always intended to work. My vision equaled happiness and fulfillment for me. It also made sense in the culture. I wasn't going to be limited to being a wife and stay-at-home mother like my mother. I was going to have a bigger life. When that life didn't work out for me, I was truly devastated. I thought my life was ruined, that I could never get over this loss. But I was wrong. I did get over it. I found a way to create a joyful, creative, fulfilling life without children, without being a research scientist, without the husband I loved. The losses will always be part of my experience, but they do not limit my ability to live a full, exciting, satisfying life.

I have never met anyone whose life has turned out as they expected—not in my personal life nor in my work with thousands of people. Some of us get caught in the pattern, like I did, that we must have some specific thing or experience in order to be happy and successful. Without that, whatever it is, we are a failure. Life may not even be worth living. That is how limiting our patterns can be.

The Past Resurfaces

Fifteen years went by without any sense of where my former husband was or how his life was unfolding when I received a letter from him. I had heard that his father had died from a Japanese friend and I had written letters of condolence both to Hiro and to his sister and sent them to the family home in Japan. The letter he sent me was brief and friendly, giving information about his father's death and news of some of our old friends. He also included in the letter:

"I have two boys and a girl, aged 13 ½, 11 ½, and 10 years, respectively. It seems that they were just babies not long ago. ... I hope we will meet some day. I have a hunch my kids are going to like you."

I was delighted by the news that he had children. He had fulfilled his vision for the family that could not happen with us; we had left each other so it could happen for him. I also liked the idea of seeing him again. We had been such good friends. At the same time, I was surprised, maybe a bit confused, about the idea of his children meeting me.

It was almost a year before Hiro and I actually met. It turned out that we both lived in the San Francisco area. He came to my home for lunch and we talked for hours. I asked questions about his perspective on our past relationship to get some reality on the accuracy of my memories. One of the things he said about me was, "I felt you could do no wrong." That was stunning! I had given that up, sent him away and never found that again. It was easy being with him. I thought it would be easy to restart our friendship.

When Hiro made some unflattering comments about his wife, I asked him to tell me some wonderful things about her, things that motivated him to ask her to marry him. His reply was a terse, "She asked me." It puzzled me why he would say only that. It didn't appear to me that there was any passion in his marriage and that troubled me. When I asked if she knew he was visiting me, and he said she didn't, I didn't like that at all. And I told him so. It felt sneaky and dangerous. I did not want to be in the middle.

Over a year went by after that visit before I received an email saying that Hiro wanted to bring his children; they wanted to meet me. He wrote that he had found a photograph of the two of us in one of his son's rooms. I was curious to meet them and experience his relationship with them. They came in the afternoon. The kids were now about 16, 14 and 12 years old. There was an ease and warmth between them and their father. It seemed clear that Hiro's children loved him and that he loved them. I took a photograph of the four of them together in my garden, and wondered how they experienced meeting me. As I watched them interact, I felt the constant work required in being a parent and believed that he had been a good one. It reassured me that I was also relieved that these children were not mine. My life now had no room for children.

It all comes full circle in a way, and yet I am outside of the story. At the end of our marriage I felt excluded, not good enough because I couldn't conceive, my life ruined, my interests gone. I suggested we get divorced so he could find a new wife, create a new life with kids and, even more importantly, so I could create mine. By my insistence, I realized later that I had excluded and abandoned him. And, by agreeing to the divorce, he had completed the abandonment of me that I had set up for him.

I did this again in my next long relationship, which lasted over a period of 14 years. I was asked and refused to marry my partner many times because I didn't want to repeat the same cycle of marriage and rejection that I feared might happen. In doing this, I excluded him. Eventually, after years of my refusing to commit, he excluded me from his thoughts, his interests, his confidences. Finally, after many years and intense personal work, after discovering much more about my limitations and fears, I found myself ready to create a future with him and was frustrated by his seeming lack of interest. I suggested that, if he didn't want to work on our relationship, perhaps we should separate. Once again, I set it up to be abandoned, and he took the opportunity.

When I got divorced in my twenties, I naively thought I could find the same love again that I was giving up. It came so easily with Hiro. I loved and trusted him and felt fully supported in being who I was. I thought we would spend our entire lives together. He opened the world for me and had a huge positive impact on my life. I loved him with all my heart. He was my prince, my great supporter. He always urged me to be whoever I wanted to be, to take on challenges, not to be afraid of failure, to always look for the learning and growth. He tried so hard, we both did. But in the end we were inept. We walked away from love as if it was replaceable. It turns out it wasn't.

Do I regret the divorce? No, I don't. At the time it felt critical for my survival. I know it was the right thing for me then. I do, however, regret the loss of the marriage and the love and the dream of a lifelong future. Yet I have lived an interesting life. I think the divorce enabled me to grow bigger and bolder. It was easy for me to look to Hiro for limits and breaking of limits. He was nine years older, more experienced and seemingly wise. My perception of this age and experience difference would have changed as the years went by, but it was liberating for me to be out on my own with no one to consider but myself. I have challenged myself in many ways and I have grown. I have taken risks and stretched. I have stepped beyond the apparent limits and found life exciting. I have also been alone a lot.

After the visit with his children, I did not hear from Hiro for more than four years. During those years, I traveled to Japan for two weeks to visit friends, including a three-day visit with Hiro's sister in the same Yokohama house I had stayed in when married. I have always loved and admired Mariko and it was a treat to share time with her again.

One evening we went out with two friends of Mariko's, one who spoke only Japanese and the other bilingual. We went to a restaurant serving a long list of gourmet *sakes*, and it seemed that we tried them all. The conversation at our table was a mix of English and Japanese, quite lighthearted until far into the food and *sake*. Mariko started talking about Hiro, saying that he should have stayed with me, and accusing him of being a fool. During this conversation, Mariko had lapsed totally into Japanese and her friend acted as translator.

I had spent time with Mariko and her father, together with Hiro, a number of times 20 years earlier, when I was living in Japan after the divorce. And, yes, they had encouraged us to get back together, regardless of children. But this was many years later, and now Hiro had another wife and three teenaged children. I was mystified. Sitting on *tatami* in the middle of that restaurant, surrounded by many other tables, I was the only non-Japanese. And we were both at least slightly tipsy. As I tried to explain why it had happened as it had, and as Mariko continued to bemoan that it should have been different, I remember that there were tears shed by both of us. This could be a soap opera, I thought.

The following morning, a little hungover but sober, sitting in the kitchen eating breakfast, Mariko and I had a good, long discussion about the relationship between Hiro and myself, and the painfulness and necessity of ending the marriage. I let her know that I would always be grateful for the time Hiro and I did have together and that I would always hold him with love. And I was honored that, after almost 20 years, she still held me as a friend. As with my interaction with Hiro, I felt I had no idea what was actually going on in his life now, but it did not feel good.

About 14 months after returning from Japan, I received another call from Hiro. He had moved and was now living in Palo Alto, California, and had been there for a year. In answer to my question about why he moved, he said, "It's a long story and I'll tell you more about it the next time I see you." Suddenly the conversations with Mariko seemed to have more meaning. The mystery of it all intrigued me and aroused my curiosity. The first thing that came to my mind was that he was separated or divorced.

It was a couple of months before we again had lunch and I heard at least a bit of his story about, as it turned out, a separation. He had felt deceived and lied to by both his wife and her parents. Doing the work I do, I'm always aware of the different versions of the same situation, the "he said, she said," with neither being the whole story. The thing that concerned me about the telling was the feeling of things being obscured, that information was hidden for a purpose.

Over the next few years, we saw each other occasionally, always at my home, always as old friends. The times we spent together were infrequent but always enjoyable. Then, one spring, Hiro announced that he was moving back to Japan, a country he had left forever at 19 years old. As it turned out, I also ended up moving out of the Bay Area that same summer. In his last visit, he brought a trunk full of things to give to me. Most of them items we had collected together during our many trips, over 30 years earlier. He wanted them to have a good home and he said, "What better home than with you?"

So once again we went our separate ways. More than eight years went by. I had some vague thoughts of another trip to Japan to visit old friends and possibly also Hiro and his sister. Then, in the early winter, I received an email from Hiro's daughter, Anne. She introduced herself and wrote: "I wanted to let you know that my father passed away January 6th from pancreatic cancer." He was nine years older than I, but still young, and I was stunned. She also wrote that she would like to talk with me, an idea that intrigued me.

The meeting with Anne didn't happen for another three years. She must have been around 30 years old by then. She picked me up at the airport on one of my regular trips to the Bay Area and we drove to a nearby coffee shop to talk. Walking with her from the car, I made some remark about her parents' divorce. She quickly clarified, "They were never married." Again I was stunned. This was the beginning of many revelations.

We talked for hours. She asked me questions about when Hiro and I met, married, divorced and our time together more recently. And she answered my questions. This is the story in a nutshell; she told it to me in bits and pieces: Hiro and her mother had met and gotten pregnant unexpectedly. Hiro had felt trapped, but had done the honorable thing and stayed to father the child, and the next one, and the last one, which Anne was. When she would ask her father at various times why he didn't marry her mother, he told her, "Why would I marry someone I don't like?" As she put it, hers was a totally dysfunctional family.

There were many details shared. I think Anne suspected that Hiro and I had been having some kind of romantic affair after the separation, which I made clear had not happened. She said he was always so happy when he returned from visiting me. And this is the kicker—Anne told me that he always referred to me as his wife and my siblings as his brothers-in-law and sister-in-law until the day he died. Hearing this, I felt another loss and great sadness.

Even over the last few years, when he had left his relationship and we were meeting occasionally, he could not be open with me about his life or his feelings. Having joked decades earlier (while still trying to figure out the future) about reconnecting in our senior years, I was curious if we could become a couple again. At that point neither of us was in a relationship and we seemed to enjoy each other's company. I made some suggestions, but he did not seem interested. I realize now that he was in hiding, perhaps ashamed of his choices, and unwilling or unable to open himself to more than limited friendship.

I had sent him away with the admonition to find a new wife and have the children he longed for. He had the children, but apparently refused to get a new wife. He loved his children and even changed his work so he could be the primary parent. But he hadn't found a new love.

Hearing all this from his daughter, I again felt that I had made a good choice for myself those many years ago. It seemed that Hiro had gotten stuck in the loss of the relationship and had never fully recovered.

His daughter even shared with me that he had felt like a failure in life. He had never been able to let go of the past, move on and create a new life that he loved.

This meeting was a great gift for me. It was like closing the circle. I think it was also a gift for his daughter, since I, the ex-wife, had been a presence in her life without knowing it.

From the time of that meeting onward, I have felt that if Hiro and I had stayed together, it would have been me he would have ended up resenting, the lack of children a constant loss and unhealed wound. I, by making the choice I did, fortunately escaped with my life wide open in front of me and into what, before we had divorced, had been unimaginable adventures.

Outside the Norm

I have no children and no grandchildren. I have only one niece and no nephews. I've never been to a PTA meeting or had a parent-teacher meeting or helped with homework or school projects or cheered for my child at a soccer game. I never even knew when school was in session or on vacation; apparently the schools don't seem to feel this is worthy of space in the newspaper because all parents already know. I missed all that and lots more. I never knew what it was to love my own children, and nurture them, and watch my children grow and evolve as they became their own people. I would have enjoyed that. But now I can't imagine it ever being a part of my life. My life took another path.

As I shared earlier, I do have a godchild, Courtney, my niece. When she was a child, we lived far apart—she in Michigan and I in California—and we rarely saw each other. I think we both missed out because of the distance. She was an only child and her few cousins, aunts and uncles all lived far away. I really enjoyed it when she came to visit as a teenager without her parents and we spent our time together talking, cooking and shopping. Now that she is an adult and married and has a child of her own, we have had many in-depth conversations, especially when she suffered her own experiences of *missed motherhood.*

Childless by choice or by circumstance, women without children experience life in a separate orbit from those with children. Parents are busy caring for and having fun with their children and families; they hang out with other families with children; and they often have careers as well as taking care of the home. For me, it seemed as though once a friend became a parent, it was easy to lose connection. It started with the arrival of the first baby who, rightfully, consumed vast amounts of time and attention. The amazement and involvement of the parents in the ever-continuing development and newly-discovered capabilities of their children as they grew consumed their attention and their sharing. It was common to drift apart.

I never felt jealous of women with children like some infertile women do. I think it's because the pain of my loss had been so dire, and my resulting choice so absolute and lifesaving. I always felt happy they had created the family they wanted and that I had found a way to escape my loss and go on to create an interesting and satisfying life.

I did feel the loss of friendship that happened when friends had their children and their energy and attention for others became severely limited. This was another loss. It seemed inevitable. But I found friends, married or not, who, like me, had no children. It happened. We created our own way of life—outside of the norm. We had more freedom and fewer limitations on our time, resources and plans. So it worked. As we all got older and children left home to go to school or work, people who were parents became more available and interested. Now they were freer as well; that is, until the grandchildren started arriving. Oh, those new babies, the grandson or granddaughter, were so compelling that they grabbed attention once again. My friends now became doting grand-parents, luxuriating in the time spent with these beautiful new souls.

I know now that many women *with* children have also experienced *missed motherhood*—maybe more than once—just like I did. And many of them never had the chance to openly grieve or talk about it or even let people know. It's highly likely that they were counseled to move on, to put it behind them, forget about it and have another child. Or perhaps they were told to be grateful they already had a child or children. But I've found in my work that they don't forget, regardless of how many children they do have. They remember. And the remembering is often vital to them, because no one else knows or remembers. If they don't hold onto the loss, it will be as if that pregnancy never happened. These women can also feel outside the norm.

In interviewing women for this book, I found them all eager to talk about their personal experiences of *missed motherhood*. No one turned me down. For many of them, it was the first time they had ever fully considered or shared about the experiences. Often, at the end of the interview, or sometime later, they would remark that the talking, the sharing, had shifted something in them and moved them to a more peaceful place. It helped me as well. I came to realize how normal *missed motherhood* actually is, how in the mainstream. So many women have experienced one or more forms of it and yet they, like me, didn't know it was so widespread.

Mother's Day can be a difficult time for women without children. A lot of us sidestep the celebrations unless we are honoring our own mother. In church on that day, the minister often asks all the mothers to stand and be honored. Those of us who have tried and failed to become mothers, or have chosen not to have children, become visible and vulnerable as we sit, left out of the celebration. Many childless women avoid the humiliation by staying home that day. But it isn't just church. I remember taking my mother to lunch one Mother's Day maybe 15 years ago, along with my sister and a friend, all of us childless except Mom. The waitress came to our table with long-stemmed red roses to give to each mother. Before she presented the rose, she wanted to confirm that we were mothers. When the three of us said we were not, she pulled the rose back. But I was not willing to be excluded anymore. I couldn't remain silent. Without thinking, I remember saying, "We are not mothers, but we are women and we want a rose as well." I think she was shocked, but graciously gave one to each of us.

Over ten years ago, realizing that Mother's Day was approaching and not wanting to endure it again, I collaborated with the minister of my church to create a service called "Honoring the Feminine." To be held on Mother's Day, the ceremony was inclusive and acknowledged the creativity of women of all situations and ages. That service is now on the Internet and in the "Resource" section of this book for all to utilize. I want to see more community experiences like that—experiences that recognize and honor *missed motherhood* as well as motherhood.

There were occurrences in my life, starting with the declaration of infertility, that I didn't like at all. They left me traumatized. I certainly suffered. At times, I was at a loss for what to do and I stumbled around a lot. I could have held onto the belief that life wasn't fair or that I was a victim, but somehow I realized that it wouldn't help me survive the trauma and live a fulfilling life.

Perceiving that there was an array of possibilities available to me was frequently challenging. I made conscious, and unknowingly unconscious, choices that other women may not have found inviting or even acceptable. Many years later, after experiencing and coming to understand more about the long-term impacts of a choice I made (and if time travel were possible), I might have acted differently. But I didn't have that luxury. I did, however, have time to explore the options available then, and to consider them as best I could before deciding. Now, there are no choices that I regret. I am satisfied that I made the best choice I could in each of those challenging situations. There are situations where I wished the available and/or perceived options were different. Regardless, I am grateful that I took action, that I made clear choices, that I did not linger too long in doubt, that I stepped forward into possibility and took the risks.

Despite the varying challenges, I was able to move through the maze of what were, at times, conflicting and confusing options to create a life of adventure, creativity, satisfaction and passion. It just wasn't at all the life I imagined it would be. I missed out on experiences I had thought were essential, especially creating my own family, raising my children and enjoying the delights of being a grandmother. But now, late in life, I realize that I have never met anyone who has lived the life they expected they would live. In my case, there always seemed to be twists and turns, upsets and victories that, when faced head-on, didn't allow me to be bored. Rather, they often opened opportunities that previously were invisible, unavailable—maybe even undesirable—but, when I stepped into them, provided surprising growth, pleasure and connection.

Looking Back With Gratitude

After all these decades of living, I look back on my life with gratitude that somehow I had the perspective, beliefs and support that I had. I realize that I lucked out! I know now, after all the work I have done with myself, and in working with others as a teacher and coach, that in addition to whatever innate personality we are born with, we also are unconsciously imprinted and molded by the environment in which we spent our early years to hold beliefs that determine how we view life. Those unconscious and conscious beliefs are powerful factors in how we approach challenges. In my early childhood experiences, through very little doing of my own, I acquired and was taught an approach to life issues that supported me through the difficult times. Other women have not necessarily been as lucky.

Despite that extended, dark, depressive, suicidal time in my twenties, after being told that I could never have my own children and other ways of becoming a parent were off the table in my marriage, I've generally considered myself an optimist. By that I mean I look for the best options that seem possible in any situation.

In my family, there were clear rules, limitations, chores and high standards of excellence. It forced me to be creative in coming up with alternate ideas that could satisfy the set parameters. Early on, I learned the art of negotiating and it has served me well throughout my life. It forced me to look at situations from a number of different perspectives and consider the options for everyone involved.

My parents empowered me to create ways to get what I wanted. A story I love to share is asking my father for a bicycle when I was about eight years old. "I think that is a great idea," he said "Now we have to figure out how you are going to earn the money to buy one." With his help I created one of my many little businesses. I think this one involved making corsages with my father's prize begonias and selling them to the neighborhood women to wear to church. He took me to the bank and we opened a savings account in which I regularly deposited whatever I earned. Once I had about $15 in the bank, Dad said, "Okay, you now have enough for a down payment, so let's go buy the bicycle.

You can continue making payments until it is paid off." I remember that bike well. It was blue with white stripes and balloon tires, and it was mine. That Christmas, my gift from my parents was the return of my bankbook with my total down payment inside. To this day, that is the most memorable Christmas gift I ever received as a child. And it wasn't just my father; my mother also had a "can do" attitude. How could I not have the same?

I was taught about making my own decisions. When asking for permission to do something I wanted to do, I frequently had to come up with a list of pros and cons as I saw them, certainly if there was any risk involved. Then I had to talk it over and come to my own conclusion and defend it. Most of the time, I got to do what I wanted. Sometimes, I even talked myself out of my own proposal.

My father loved his work and my mother championed being a stay-at-home mom. The message I received as a child was go after what you love. There was no question about whether any one of the four children was going to college—it was assumed and expected. There would have been a fight if we didn't go. But where we went and what we studied was up to us. Even as a teenager I wanted to be a research scientist, I wanted to discover what was previously unknown. Encouraging me to go after my passion (and once I had saved enough money), my father took me to New York City to buy a used medical microscope. I spent many happy hours studying specimens I found in nature.

While I had always held the vision that I would have a husband and children—but only two, not four as in my childhood family—I totally rejected the idea of staying home as too limiting. I always wanted to work as well as be a mother.

We were a middle class family living in the suburbs of New York City, where my father was an executive in a manufacturing company. All was not rosy and money was tight, but there was encouragement to go after what you love. Years later, reading a genealogy of the Comstock family, I found what is purported to be the Comstock family coat of arms. The motto is in Welsh and, when translated, reads: "Not Wealth, but Contentment." I think that fits.

My life has not turned out at all how I thought it would when I was a child or young adult, but looking back over all that I have done and experienced, I do feel content. I was able to deal with the difficult challenges that life presented to me—and that I created for myself—and build a life that encompassed adventures that were unimaginable as a child, fulfillment of childhood dreams that seemed impossible and work that I have pursued with passion. There are experiences that I would have liked that I didn't have, and maybe still will have.

Surprisingly, remembering that I wanted to die rather than go through life childless, I cannot regret that I never had a child. Now, at this time in my life, I cannot imagine ever having been a mother. Thankfully, I was able to release that dream, choose to live another way and build the life that I've had. Taking all that I've had to contend with in my own life, the choices I was able to make, the support I found and the way my life developed, I have the opportunity now to share what I have learned and expand the options for others. Through my work over the last 25 years, I have been honored to begin sharing with and supporting other women who have *missed motherhood* in healing the pain and creating fulfilling lives for themselves.

Part Two

DIFFERENT CHOICES, VARIED PATHS

It is human nature to want to believe that we can control our life and make happen whatever we desire. In each of our lives there are many things we can and do control. Eventually we come to realize that absolute control is not part of being human. But we can always control the choices we make, the action we take and what we choose to do with circumstances that come our way so that we create a life that brings us satisfaction and joy.

Other Women's Stories

What I have discovered over many years of friendships, teaching and coaching with other women is that *missed motherhood* happens in different and varied ways in a woman's life. It happens frequently and is only minimally shared. In working on this book, I found it difficult to find any woman who had not had an experience of what I have defined as *missed motherhood* at some point in her life. While it is quite obvious that when a woman does *not* have any children (either by choice or by chance), she fits into at least one of the five categories of *missed motherhood,* it is an unknown for women who have children.

As I shared the topic of this book with any woman who was interested, I uncovered stories. I also found a willingness, an eagerness, in the women to share their stories. For almost all of the women whose stories are included here, they had never shared their *missed motherhood* experience beyond the mere facts, if even that, before I interviewed them. I asked them what happened, what they felt and thought then and now, how they were supported and how they would have liked to have been supported. And I listened.

I was often surprised by the complexity, the various twists and turns involved. My interest in hearing each story, my focused listening without comment or advice, created a space for these women to explore within themselves and express in words what had been held within, with no place to go. Allowing all the time necessary to express everything they had to say, surprisingly, often took less than a few hours. All the thoughts and feelings that had been held close, suppressed, hidden even from themselves at times, unshared often for decades, were released into the air. It was often a transformative experience. It was always an honor for me to be their witness.

The losses that a woman experiences as a result of her own choices are often the least well-received by others and are therefore the hardest to share—the choice not to have any children, or to terminate a pregnancy, or to wait for the right time that never comes. The recognition and sharing of those losses is often interpreted as regret, that the choice they made was wrong, rather than as a recognition of what the choice actually entailed.

What interested me about all of these women and their stories was, regardless of the challenge that *missed motherhood* presented to them, they had found a way over the years to bring healing to the loss, integrate the experiences into their lives and create lives that were fulfilling. They had made choices to deal with whatever loss that had incurred. Mostly, they had done the healing work alone, without direction or knowledge of how they could be most effective, or anyone with whom they could share the depth of their experience.

The interviews were recorded and I wrote the stories based on what the women said. Each woman reviewed and edited the written story so they felt it accurately reflected their experience, and they each chose a name that was not their own. I introduce these women at the start of their story and then they speak for themselves. The final segment, "Barbara's Story," is not derived from an interview, but was written by my sister, Barbara Comstock.

Carol's Story

Carol always thought she would be a good mom, and imagined having just one child. Her husband, in contrast, wanted more. So in the years before they were married, they argued back and forth about how many children they would actually have. At some point, her husband attended a presentation about world population growth. After that, they both settled on one child as their goal. Then, when Carol was ready to have children, she reflected on being an only child herself and changed her goal to two. She thought it would be great for her child to have a sibling. This is her story.

It took almost a year after we started trying before I got a rather ambiguous pregnancy test. A few days later, when my period started near the end of the workday, I was bummed that I wasn't pregnant but sensed that something was different this time. By the time I got home, I had bled through a tampon and a pad and clear through my bike shorts, chamois and all. There was so much blood that I went from being disappointed to being scared. My husband, who arrived home in the nick of time, took me to the hospital where I was eventually given a D&C to stop the bleeding. This was my first miscarriage. It was upsetting and disappointing after waiting so long and wondering if it was going to happen, but we also saw this as an auspicious event, confirming that the sperm could reach the egg.

My very next cycle, I got pregnant again. Understanding that miscarriages are common, I had no concerns about it happening again. This pregnancy was normal in every way. I was physically active, we traveled internationally and our son was born on time and perfectly normal. I quit my job and became a full-time mother.

After much discussion with other mothers and my husband, we decided that three years between siblings was the optimal interval. At two years old, my son was so adorable I couldn't imagine not wanting another child. I became pregnant at exactly the right time. This time I was spotting at five-and-a-half weeks and got a horrible case of gastroenteritis that seemed to last until I was 14 weeks pregnant. But once I had an ultrasound showing the heartbeat at six weeks, and another one at 19 weeks showing a well-developed fetus, no one seemed concerned about the pregnancy. We couldn't decide on a girl's name, but quickly agreed on a name if it was a boy.

I was 22 ½ weeks pregnant when I noticed a few drops of blood on the floor as I showered. I didn't think there was anything to be concerned about, but just to be safe, I decided to have it checked out. At the hospital I learned that my cervix was already dilated, there was nothing they could do about it, and that I would go into labor within the next few days. At 22 ½ weeks, the baby was too undeveloped for any possibility of survival. However surprising it was, the way they described the situation was so definitive that both my husband and I felt relief that we didn't need to make any decision. The result had been decided for us.

That night the contractions began. The labor was long, but very weak, and it felt like I could turn it on or off just by standing up or lying down. I could feel the baby kicking the entire time. He was alive and I knew he was going to die. My body was forcing it to happen and there was nothing I could do about it. As soon as he was born, my husband took our son into his arms and said, "I love you," so that he would hear it before he died a few minutes later.

They did not whisk him away like they do with viable premature births, but allowed us to be with him. Our midwife brought tiny clothes handmade by a local church group, made sure we had photos and hand prints and helped us perform many of the traditional rituals of live births, like clamping and cutting the cord and weighing and bathing him. She helped us dress him and prepared a beautiful little box with a blanket and pillow.

We took our new son home to grieve as a family with our first son. We acknowledged him as our child and treated his death as the loss of a family member. We decorated the inside of his box with photos of the people who loved him and put flowers from our garden inside and out. Our older son gave him a toy and we tucked him in with the stuffed animal that we had bought for him early in my pregnancy. The grief was overwhelming. We knew he was dead and we were not responsible for him anymore, but it was difficult to let go. When the funeral home picked him up, I felt I was abandoning him.

In addition to the support I received from my husband, I was able to openly share my loss with my mothers' group and also with the much older women in my ice skating group who had shared their own similar pregnancy losses years earlier. A big question for me was *How do I move on?* Knowing that others had successfully healed themselves and enjoyed a good life, and that many of these women had gone on to have other children, allowed me to feel more normal and have hope for my future.

At the time of this son's death, one reassuring thought was, *This one was not meant to be.* And since our goal had been to have a baby, not necessarily *this* baby, I felt less distressed than I might have. However, even though our child was born too early to survive, I later often wondered if I'd given up on him too easily. I questioned whether we had accepted what the doctors said because it was convenient.

We waited six months before trying for the next pregnancy. At nine weeks, almost exactly 12 months after our second son's premature birth, I miscarried again, in a most bloody and inconvenient fashion while on a social outing with my husband's workmates. After the miscarriage, I felt partly relieved, questioning whether I really wanted another child, and decided for a time I was done.

After some months, I came to realize I was not ready to give up and became pregnant again. Now I was concerned that I could miscarry. In the dating ultrasound at nine weeks that was now warranted by my history, they found that the embryo had not developed. There was no heartbeat. I felt alone and vulnerable and just wanted to sob, but there was no point. As with my other pregnancies, I had felt ill from about six weeks so I just wanted to be done with it. I was tired of being sick, tired of being pregnant. Rather than go through another bloody miscarriage, I agreed to a D&C the following week.

For five years I had been working at home part-time and feeling isolated. Now, if I wasn't going to have more babies, I questioned, *What I was going to do?* When I finally decided to stop trying to have another child and start working again, I immediately felt great—almost like turning a light switch. We had missed what we felt was the optimal interval between siblings. I was 38 years old and wondering if the losses were my body's way of telling me my eggs were too old.

I started a new job and quickly felt so much better than being at home that I knew I was finished trying to have another child. At work I celebrated the first August in years I had not experienced a trip to the hospital and a failed pregnancy. I had more energy and could once again plan for the future. I was glad I had one child, didn't regret any of the pregnancies. I was happy I was past all of that. I've been working for three years now and am happy with what I am doing. I am now also loving all of the physical activity that I wasn't able to do when I was pregnant or looking after a young baby, and my husband and I have been doing lots of running, bike riding and skiing that were not possible when I was in the pregnancy/miscarriage cycle.

Around this time, we began to realize that our son, who was now four-and-a-half years old, wasn't interacting as much as other children his age. He didn't seem to follow many of the implicit social rules, like looking at us when we spoke or answering questions directly. Our pediatrician began to mention Asperger's Syndrome and ADHD, but we didn't want to hear it. Being a mother of a child who didn't interact with other children was isolating. We didn't have the same feeling of community that other families do. Ironically, that doubled the challenge for us, because we were less likely to get a break. Thankfully, over the years as our son has been able to develop friendships, our feelings of isolation have passed.

Chloe's Story

At ten years old, as the eldest of six children, Chloe was already mothering her younger siblings. By the age of 12, Chloe made the decision that she didn't want to have any children of her own when she grew up and she had announced this decision to her mother. Her commitment never changed. Here is her story.

At the age of 20 I became pregnant and quickly planned an abortion. There was no question about it. Later, in my mid-twenties, I married a man who had a vasectomy so there was no question of getting pregnant. After we divorced, as a member of a spiritual community in my thirties, I was offered the opportunity to have a tubal ligation and I did. I remember feeling a huge amount of relief and freedom after I had it done. Now I couldn't get pregnant and this supported my continuing decision not to have children.

For most of my adult life, I have felt supported in my decision. My parents didn't seem to care. Living in California, I experienced an open attitude about children—it was accepted whether you had them or not. After moving to the east coast, I began butting up against the expectation that a woman *should* have children—most women I know have them. There are no words spoken, but there is a certain amount of exclusion that seems to happen in conversations, levels of closeness and intimacy. I feel that I'm viewed as different because I don't have any children. I don't know the answer, but I do experience a certain separateness—perhaps this is as much mine as theirs.

Most of my friends who do not have children accept that as a fine choice. I believe there is more of an expectation on the east coast that women should have children. This has been surprising and somewhat hurtful, as if I'm "less than." It feels like it's back to the old days when a woman who didn't have children was seen as "barren." This is a loss. Now I'm realizing, *Oh, I don't have a family.* It's certainly out of the question at this time in my life, where before it might not have been.

By not having children, I feel I gained a lot of space and energy for my life. Being childfree has given me the opportunity to forge new territories and explore unknown paths and more space to create. Being a woman doesn't mean you have to be a mother too. Perhaps being childfree has given me the opportunity to mother in a bigger way. It's given me the time and space to mother many more children and people. Over the years, I've taught hundreds of children in school, worked in a field of education to support children and now I work to mother adults so they can resolve their childhood issues. If I had my own children, I would have been focused on them.

What I've lost is the experience of conceiving, birthing and having an incredible, intense relationship with one being, that child which I haven't had. My mother often spoke about that. One time in my forties, I recall her saying, "You wouldn't understand, there's nothing like mother love." That was the first time I thought, *Oh, I wouldn't understand.* The first time I realized that I might have lost out. It was a surprise. I was confused. I thought maybe I made the wrong choice; or that maybe that choice wasn't conscious, that it was reaction to childhood. So I've been willing to explore it.

In my forties I finally grieved the loss of the child I had conceived and aborted—out of the blue a wave of grief overtook me. I acknowledged that little being and spoke with it and explained I was sorry and very much felt its presence. I had a clairvoyant reading and I was told: "This baby being is in your field and is pulling on your uterus. It might be good to suggest to this baby being that you're happy to have this little being in your life, but it must be as a guide. You will not be bringing it into this world." I did do this.

Recently, on Mother's Day, the minister had all mothers come forward and stand in front and be honored. Only four or five women were left seated and I was one of them. It was humiliating. After the service, I spoke with other women, both standing and sitting, and it seems we were all horrified. I never went back to that church. The experience triggered another grief cycle for me and I suddenly became aware of the little baby being. I felt that he/she was guiding me to move through the grief and let go.

Again I spoke with the little being. Since I have a fibroid, I wanted to be clear that I'm not bringing a child in. I believe that there are unconscious forces that are so powerful and so strong that no matter how much work and consciousness I bring to this issue, I still feel that there are deeper layers I haven't penetrated yet. It's in our DNA as women that our bodies are built to bring children into being and when we tell our body *No,* it gets confused.

Mary's Story

It was the Sixties in New York City. Mary was 19 and still living at home. Birth control was almost non-existent and abortion was illegal when she found herself pregnant at the very beginning of a new relationship. She was shocked and bewildered and never even told the man. Luckily, she had good friends who were savvy and connected with knowledgable people; they hooked her up with an abortionist. Mary never knew whether the man had any medical training, but she was desperate. There was no acceptance or support at that time for children born outside of marriage and no possibility in her mind of anything but abortion. There were no other choices. This was to be her secret for many years to come. Here is Mary's story.

I was directed to the home of an apparently affluent couple on Long Island, where I spent the weekend. They inserted some instrument into my vagina and then told me to get up and go out in the yard and pull weeds and walk around. I was so desperate I never even asked if they had any medical credentials. I spent the night there and, within 24 hours, started hemorrhaging into a container they had left for me in the bathroom. When I finished, they took the container away. I was petrified about what was happening in my body and wondered if I was going to be okay—it didn't feel like it was legitimate medical care. It was fear and trauma. When my friend came the following day to pick me up, I experienced tremendous relief that it was over. For weeks after, I was hyper-vigilant about my body, watching for any signs of trouble.

Four years later, I got pregnant with the man I later married. I wanted the child and was very excited. The father was a free spirit and happy about it as well. At almost three months, I started bleeding and he had to rush me to the hospital, where they confirmed I was miscarrying and did a D&C. My partner was compassionate, the nurses were kind and I felt supported and embraced. What I told myself was that the miscarriage was retribution for having had an abortion—something wrong was done to my body in that abortion and now the D&C had fixed it.

They told me not to get pregnant for three months, but, almost immediately—within six weeks—I was pregnant again. I was in shock, ecstatic and wondering, *How did that happen?* It had a different feeling this time, like everything was going to be okay. The pregnancy was flawless and our daughter was born. Later we had a second daughter. I was totally enamored with pregnancy and giving birth—I loved it all. I was in bliss and totally adored my babies. Caregiving was harder. Once the babies were born, I never thought about the previous experiences.

Women should be able to choose and should have safe, compassionate and educated support for whatever they choose when they find themselves pregnant. There are choices that we make. I feel I made good choices that were obvious to me and I have no regrets. I would have loved to have had emotional support during the time of my abortion, someone to physically be there with me. It would have been great to have had a caregiver, like a midwife, who was educated and knowledgable. We should have control over our reproductive rights and the trajectory of our lives. It's a personal issue and an economic issue.

I've never talked with my two adult daughters about my abortion or miscarriage. When one of my daughters was volunteering for Planned Parenthood, I think I mentioned to her that I had to have an abortion when it was illegal and I supported what she was doing, but there was no discussion beyond saying that we could never go back to that. Neither of my daughters, who are now in their thirties, have children.

Even now, over 40 years later, it surprises me that the thought of standing up in public and just saying, "I had an abortion," brings up anxiety. There's a little vibe still that we shouldn't talk about it. I feel gratitude that we can be talking about it together now.

Kimberly's Story

Having her own children was always central to Kimberly's vision for her life. Her family was very close with siblings, aunts, uncles, cousins and grandparents. She thought that having children was the way it was—the next generation always coming. Seeing some of her older cousins getting divorced when she was still in her twenties, and knowing that was not what she wanted for herself, Kimberly decided to wait for the perfect partner. She also realized that, as a teacher of young children all day, she was not yet eager to come home to her own children. This is Kimberly's story.

I postponed any thoughts of children into my early thirties and then started realizing that finding the perfect partner was not that easy. Some friends were having children and I thought that if I'm going to have them, I'd better get going. I considered adopting, as some of my single friends did. I also thought about having a baby on my own, but, as an unmarried teacher, I didn't know how I would explain my pregnancy to my young students. I also considered becoming a foster parent a number of times in my life.

In my late thirties, I married a man who was younger. He wasn't the perfect partner, but I thought, *Now I can have kids.* When I became pregnant, he was not excited about it. Feeling very pregnant at three months, I was alone at a routine check-up when the ultrasound found no heartbeat. It was a major shock since there had been no indication of trouble. I'll never forget that day. As I drove home, I was crying. The next day I returned with my husband to have a D&C. That was difficult emotionally, but, thinking there would be another chance to have a baby, I didn't grieve for long.

As time went by, I realized, *This isn't the relationship I want,* and got a divorce. I came to rationalize the miscarriage as "for the best"— that it was not the right time or right marriage. Again I considered adoption and actually took some action to become a foster parent.

In my forties, I met the man who is my husband now. I put on hold the idea of fostering, since the beginning of a marriage is not the right time. When, at 47, I wanted to get pregnant, the doctor encouraged me.

"If you're going to do it, do it now," he said, without even mentioning that my eggs were probably dead. I never got pregnant.

My husband prefers to be childfree and is not eager to adopt or foster children. In the last year, realizing my age, I've been asking myself, *Do I really want children?*

At 50, my reality is that I have no children, no family and I will not have grandchildren. If I'd really wanted a child, I realize that I would have changed my situation or not let it limit my choices. I made those choices and sometimes I regret them. I know I am not going to adopt, but foster care or being with kids in other ways does not have a time limit. There is a need for people to help other people. I can connect to kids through mentoring, but the question is how much time and commitment I want to put towards that.

Throughout my life I have taught many children in kindergarten through third grade. I can feel the love. I often get to see them for over six years. Some come back or send wonderful letters, but usually I don't know what happens to them. Now that I realize I'm not going to have my own child, I look at my students differently. I'm more mothering, noticing the children who need extra help. I enjoy their youngness. Maybe this is the gift for me.

Part of me wishes that I could say, "I didn't want kids and I'm happy as a clam!" I made the choice to postpone and then got caught in the circumstances of life and ended up with no children. I do have lots of friends and they became family. I have had more energy for friendship than they have. I also had a lot of energy for me. I would at times question myself: *Do I want it to be different?*

In our culture, there is so much emphasis on mothers and children. So much socializing is driven by children playing with other women's children and then the parents becoming friends as well. At times I find it hard to feel a part of what others are doing.

When I was younger, my friends were childless as well. Now, in some social groups, everyone has children and I feel different, separate. Maybe it's me. I could have been more actively involved with friends with children. Initially it was because of the pain of loss. Even now I still feel loss when I'm with families with children. I feel I should have had children.

New people in my life always ask, "How many kids do you have?" It feels sad—no children, no grandchildren. I have nothing to report. It isn't spoken, but I feel they are sad for me as they would be for a sick friend.

When I hear about another woman who hasn't had a child, I always want to know her story. Some women without children are much more at peace than I am. My willingness to look at all the options has kept the question open for me without resolution. If I had married a man who had children, that would have solved it for me. There was a time when I wanted to bear the child, but what I really want is a sense of family.

In relationships there are good times and hard times that you work through, and the relationship develops and deepens. This must also be true for parents and children. In school I have had loving connections with children while they are in my class, but, when they leave my class, the relationship changes. I miss the depth that develops over the long-term.

I have thought about my pregnancy and miscarriage a lot throughout my life. When I did a workshop about losses, I relived it. When I was pregnant, I had a vision that it was a girl and I had named her Denali. It was sad—the image of that child dying. As a result of that work, I felt a shift happening, a letting go. Overall, I think that forgetting has been my strategy to deal with loss and it's interesting how the sadness has resurfaced at various times in my life. I can see I could have talked about the loss more. Maybe it's like an illness that you don't want to talk about, don't know how to acknowledge, and the sadness you don't want. I've had lower back pain for a long time and, in talking about all this now, I am feeling something releasing in my back.

Afterword: *Ten years later, I spoke with Kimberly again and she shared how things had been for her during that time:*

When we first spoke, I was 50. Now I'm 60, and I'm at my happiest. Finally I'm getting it. My husband and I *are* the family and I'm at my most content. I focus on the good news. I feel happy for my friends who have children and I love their kids. At the same time, I wish I had more friends without children who feel more like I have. There should be a website: "Oops, I forgot to have kids!" A support group of other women in a similar situation would have been helpful.

It's easy to mourn what we don't have. I have to ask myself: *If I could have a child right now, would I take it on?* If I'd gotten pregnant at 47, my child would have been eight years old when I retired from teaching and only 13 years old now. It's hard to imagine.

There's something in me that I want to pass on to another generation. I remember my father putting his hand on my shoulder as we walked and I felt such love and security, and I realize I have no child of my own to do that with. Now that I am retired, I am reaching out into the community to create more sharing and mentoring relationships with women, both older and younger, and their children. I feel purposeful as I walk toward new experiences. I would love to witness a birth, and that is still possible.

Bella's Story

Bella always knew she wanted to have children and be a mother, although she never imagined what she would face trying to get what she wanted. Married at 28 years old and pregnant after ten months, Bella miscarried in February of 1992. Here, Bella shares her story.

The memories of how my body, emotions, intellect and spirit felt that fateful day when I lost my first child are as vivid as if it happened yesterday. People minimized my loss as, "Well, honey, it's a sign something was wrong." Or, "It's better it happened now and not later." No one, not even my family, acknowledged that I lost a child. I didn't seek help with my grief, I just "got it together" and focused on the future.

The next pregnancy ended in July, 1992. I was not even aware of the pregnancy until it was almost over. This loss left me angry and confused. I didn't know what was wrong with me. My faith was rocky as I tried to understand why I was being punished by God. Why couldn't I hold onto my children? I felt helpless. I had never failed at anything I set out to do in my life. Once again, no one acknowledged the loss and my grieving went untended to.

I picked up, moved on and started gathering information so I could figure out how to fix myself. Pregnant again in February, 1993, after two miscarriages, we decided to contain our excitement for the first weeks. In March, when the same familiar feelings started, I knew this was another miscarriage happening. I withdrew into my grief, longing for all my lost babies to return to my body. Unaccustomed to failure, I had now failed three times.

I realized I needed help. Unbeknownst to others, I was drowning in my sorrow. I put on a stiff upper lip and moved on from life tragedies. I had learned in childhood, as a "military brat," not to waste time missing what we left behind. This skill was not serving me in this situation. I needed to acknowledge and grieve these "deaths" that were within my body.

Through personal growth work accomplished in the intensive weeklong Hoffman Process, I was led back to my true self and felt freed from the limits of conditional love and false negative beliefs about who I had to be. I felt reborn and renewed. I loved my new sense of wholeness and freedom from the inner pain and torment of loss.

In the next few months I didn't get pregnant, so, later that fall, we consulted our doctor. He put me on Clomid, which immediately resulted in a painful overreaction, enlarging my ovaries to the size of large grapefruits. After recovering from that episode, I was referred to an endocrinologist at UCLA for repeated hormone injections, which resulted in at least two eggs being released. I received more shots to sustain the pregnancy. The doctor said it might be twins. I did not want my husband to suffer another disappointment, so I decided not to tell him until I knew for sure. Ten days later, the bleeding started. I grieved silently.

Deciding to do a full workup, the doctor injected dye into my fallopian tubes. There was a one-in-3,000 chance of an allergic reaction that could cause peritonitis, which the doctor blithely waved aside. Two weeks later, while travelling across the country, I became incredibly sick with fever and pain. It kept getting worse. I flew back home and was diagnosed with peritonitis that was so severe I could have died if they had not caught it in time.

In April of 1994, we were in Paris. After a fabulous evening celebrating our fourth anniversary, I recognized the moment of conception. After the doctor verified the pregnancy, we were blissed out for days. Then, four weeks later, driving home from a business meeting, I nearly passed out from incredibly sharp pains, but no bleeding. My doctor was informed and, when the pain returned, tests revealed another miscarriage—still without any bleeding. At work the next week, I again experienced excruciating pain, but still no blood. I thought, *I'll be all right, I can handle this. We know it's a miscarriage, I've done this four times.* But it wasn't a normal miscarriage. When they did an ultrasound, they found that my uterus was empty—it was a tubal pregnancy and I needed immediate surgery. The two-week delay in diagnosis had resulted in excessive internal bleeding, which could have been fatal. Even after emergency surgery, I continued to bleed from my naval. I could never go through that again. The doctor kept saying, "You are so lucky to be alive." None of us were grieving the loss of the baby, we were just worried about my life.

After this experience, I sought therapy and I learned much more about myself—my focused determination, my willingness to suffer, my need to "hold it all together" even if it threatened my life, my inability to care and nurture myself, my lack of boundaries. I minimized the pain, incredibly insensitive to my physical limits. I put myself through hell and kept going. I trusted others, not myself, to tell me what I was feeling and what was true.

I wanted a baby for me, for my husband, for my parents and siblings, for the world. Up to this point I was willing to do anything, suffer anything, pay any amount of money, to birth a baby. Having life within was a miracle, an awesome experience. But now, that miracle of life was starkly contrasted with death, both housed in the very same place; it was the power to create life without the power to stop death.

We started discussing the question, "Are we sure we really want children after all this?" I was scared to become pregnant, ambivalent at best. I reluctantly went along with my husband's preference not to use protection and see what would happen. I only had one tube at this point, and it might have been damaged, so my chances of pregnancy were slim. I went three years without a pregnancy.

In January of 1998, I had a premonition that I was pregnant. Tests confirmed it. Extremely hopeful once again, at nine weeks we learned it was another ectopic (tubal) pregnancy. The doctor gave me the choice of trying to save or remove my last tube. After seven pregnancies and eight lost souls, I couldn't take anymore. The war was over. I surrendered. He removed both tubes and I was done.

I am a giver. Not being able to give the gift of life to my husband, my family or myself was a huge loss. A unique gift of being a woman is bringing forth life. I wanted that experience so badly, and it was not going to happen for me.

Finally, I had to acknowledge to myself that I was a mother even though all my "children" had died and others didn't acknowledge it. From the first moment of conception, I knew life was within me. I sensed their genders and named each one. I had felt the thrill of that miracle and the physical and emotional changes that occurred, even during brief, seven-to-ten-week pregnancies. Now I had to close that chapter of my life.

There had been so much loss—loss of control of my body, loss of connection to faith since I felt punished by God, loss of life, loss of wholeness and health, loss of connection to being fully alive, loss of innocence—and I felt responsible for my husband's losses. We had suffered secretly, in silence, without the knowledge or support of others.

In May of 1998, encouraged by a grief counselor, we created a ritual, a ceremony to remember the children lost, acknowledge our shattered dreams and hopes, express our honest grief, bind our hearts together and acknowledge our losses in our community of family and friends. In the memorial garden we had created, we claimed each one of those babies as our own, we buried mementos and we read letters we had written to the babies, to each other, to the family. We allowed our grief to be seen by our community and to be supported and nurtured. I was also comforted by the stories of other women who had responded to our memorial announcement by sharing their losses, which validated that I wasn't alone and that it was perfectly natural and normal to acknowledge our "children," even if they were never birthed.

With the support of therapy and others who shared their journeys with me, I allowed myself to acknowledge, claim, grieve and share the loss. I found peace with the fact that I had no children here on Earth. I had given up the dream of motherhood and turned my attention and energy to supporting others in their healing. I became a teacher of the same work that had helped me, years earlier, in freeing myself from suffering and in finding self-love and wholeness. Finding fulfillment in work, I returned to my workaholic ways.

In 2001, six of my seven consulting clients went down in the towers on 9/11 and I was rear-ended twice by drunk drivers. I had to take time off to heal the effects of the injury to my brain. The next year, I was rear-ended twice more. I thought, *What's next?*

In 2002, I was awakened, night after night, at 3 a.m. with someone calling my name, and no one was there. So, one night, I sat up at 3 a.m., waiting for the call. When I heard it once again, I asked, "Who are you and what do you want?" What I heard was, "You're going to have a baby." I was 38 years old without any fallopian tubes. How was this going to be possible?

I called my obstetrician. It had been five years since my last tubal pregnancy. Tests showed I had the eggs of a 25-year-old, so *in vitro fertilization* (IVF) was possible. We decided to try. When they finally got the level of the hormone injections correct, four embryos were placed in my uterus and I became pregnant with twins. With IVF, I would receive progesterone injections for 12 weeks to support the pregnancy. At six weeks, one fetus stopped growing and, at ten weeks, the heartbeat of the other stopped.

Since I had been led by the voice of spirit, I went to the spirit of the baby to ask, "Why did you come?" The answer I received was, "I came to experience what it feels like to be wanted." How could it be that all those babies hadn't felt wanted? I needed to know that my uterus was sending the message of my heart. In saying goodbye, the baby spirit said to me, "Please stop your suffering and have a D&C so you won't have to go through the pain of another miscarriage." So, for the first time, I allowed the doctor to do the surgery and my body was relieved and thankful.

I felt I had wanted all the babies and they had all left, one after another, abandoning me. I needed to heal this. I went to our memorial garden the day the heart stopped to speak with the baby spirit. I asked, "Am I having another child?" The answer that came was, "Yes."

Six months later, I decided to do one more IVF with four embryos. Very early I knew it was twins and ultrasound confirmed it. I felt one was a girl and one a boy. At 11 weeks I was doing great and so were the babies. Suddenly something didn't feel right, and they found the girl's heartbeat had stopped. Afraid I would also lose my son, my doctor assured me I should be able to carry him to term. When I asked the girl's spirit why she didn't stay, she said, "There wasn't room for both of us. I just came to help him get started."

On April 12, 2004, my son was born naturally on his due date at nine pounds, four ounces, after a 36-hour labor. I was joyous. There still is a peacefulness and oneness within my being, having experienced what I wanted to experience.

Mothering comes naturally to me. Had my husband been agreeable, I would have stopped my suffering, adopted and become a mother sooner. Life takes us down different pathways than we expect. I had no idea my journey to motherhood would be like it has been. Four years ago, I divorced my son's father, changed careers and am now a life coach, activist and singer/songwriter. Although I never dreamed I would be a single mom, I have redesigned my life around being a mother. My son is nearly nine and I am immensely grateful.

Through my painful journey, I came to realize how I have struggled with failure. After becoming a mother, I uncovered a hidden shame I had been carrying of being a girl when my parents wanted a boy. Now I was able to claim my natural feminine energy and, for the first time in my life, my menstrual cycles became normal. Having a baby, I became a woman and more receptive. I am still in the process of learning to claim my femininity. I know now I do not have to suffer,

I can listen to my body and know my own truth.

Afterword: *After reading her story as written here, Bella woke up in the middle of the night, remembering a traumatic experience she had suppressed for more than a quarter of a century. She was stunned at the recollection:*

At 21, while in college, I went to the student health center because I was bleeding heavily and didn't know what was wrong. After the nurse checked out possibilities and tested me, I was shocked to learn I was nine weeks pregnant and miscarrying. I couldn't believe it, as I had just had my first sexual encounter during a summer romance and my boyfriend had "pulled out." Sexually naive, I hadn't even counted it as having sex. And I had gotten pregnant!

I remember being relieved that I was miscarrying and that I didn't have to make the difficult choice of aborting a child. I also felt sad and guilty. There I was: in a Christian college, no longer a virgin *and* I had lost a baby. I was a "bad girl." This became a deep, dark secret, even from me.

Finally I understand why, after the later miscarriages when married, I always felt that God was punishing me. Unknowingly, I felt I was being punished for the earlier shameful pregnancy, which I didn't even remember.

There is so much that has just become clear to me. For years, I was driven by my patterns, my subconscious belief systems. From the time I was born, I was made to feel that I couldn't have what I wanted, that I had to please others and that I had to be "good."

Having sex before marriage and getting pregnant had made me "bad" and unworthy. Denial is the way my family handled discrepancies: "What is happening isn't happening." "Pretend it's not happening, it will go away." Having a baby when married became a way not only to prove that I could have what I want, but also to demonstrate my goodness, femininity and worth. Not birthing a child was punishment. Unconsciously, I was battling myself.

When I accepted that I wasn't going to have a child and created the ritual experience, I began to open a space to move beyond the driving force of my patterns and listen to the guidance of spirit, and finally have a child. Now it makes sense.

Sophia's Story

In high school, after her first serious boyfriend broke off their relationship, Sophia was deeply hurt and felt worthless for a long time. That loss fed into previously existing self-worth issues. Her boyfriend had dismissed her, accusing Sophia of being "just a nice Jewish girl." Although she was an honors student and active in many school activities, her relationship to men changed. This is Sophia's story.

After high school, I began a risky, promiscuous lifestyle of attractions to "bad boys." Perhaps my behavior was a way of defying my former boyfriend; I had to prove that I wasn't such a nice girl after all. Perhaps it was a way of punishing myself—as though I did not believe I was really worthy of finding a man whom I respected and who would love me. At one point, I even had a relationship with a much older and alcoholic college professor. Maybe it was the riskiness that made it exciting.

I never had an overwhelming desire to have children. I felt strongly about being an artist and wanted my creative energy to go into my artwork. The difficulties of making a living as an artist convinced me that I did not want to be a single mother. At the time, I felt free, doing what I wanted. Unless I found a partner with whom I could settle down and who could provide some financial support, I simply would not have children. I had doubts about being married anyway. My mother had been so unhappy in her marriage, beaten down by my father's moods—I think he must have been bipolar, and she was living in fear of his anger.

I lived abroad in my late twenties, and was active in the feminist movement. It was very important for me to have a whole political movement affirm that I didn't have to be owned by a man, didn't have to be married.

In my mid-thirties, I was shocked to find myself pregnant. *Oh my god!* I thought. *This has actually happened to me—a liberated woman using birth control.* I wasn't with someone I wanted to marry. I was thankful that this hadn't happened when I was living overseas where abortion was illegal, or earlier, like one of my high school friends who had to go to Mexico to get an abortion. Telling the man involved didn't bring us any closer, but he did offer to help pay for the abortion, which was now legal, safe and performed in a clinic. I couldn't talk about it to anyone except one friend, after the fact. I felt very isolated and I moved on in life.

Eventually, I had two more abortions in similarly inappropriate relationships. Each time I just moved on. I felt sad I had aborted, but not guilty. I did not feel that I had killed a child—the fetus hadn't yet developed into a human being, it was just the size of a pea. I realized there was something wrong with my lifestyle, but I didn't want to think about it. I didn't allow myself to consider what it meant and, again, I just moved on. My closest women friends were also choosing not to have children. We thought the world was over-populated and that, in our own way, we were helping to keep the population down.

In 2000, I was living in a rural, small-town community I had grown to love, and then I had to move back to the Bay Area. I asked my yoga teacher if our yoga class could give me a blessing to help me make the transition. After my last class with the group, my teacher had me lie down on the floor and all the other people came to kneel beside me. Each person laid their hands on me and gave me an individual blessing and told me how I was loved. My body received the beautiful, warm energy from each person's hand and the love in their voice. When the ritual was over, I felt at peace, ready to make the journey ahead.

Many years later—decades, actually—in talking with a therapist about a bout of depression, I shared the impact of the breakup of my high school relationship, the later promiscuity and abortions and I started to put more of the pieces together. Out of those sessions, I decided to create a ritual for those three little beings.

I formed simple little figurines out of clay and wrapped each one in silk. I imagined the potential human beings each of them might have grown into. I could have had a daughter, just as my mother had me. My mother loved me and I had been a source of great pleasure for her. If I had done something wrong, then I wanted forgiveness—but I did not think I had done wrong. There hadn't been a choice for me—I was doing the best I could back then, coping with life. For each of the beings, I dug a hole in my yard and buried them so they were close to each other. I felt the grief. The ritual brought recognition of sadness for what had and hadn't been. After the ritual, I felt relief. I had a different relationship with them. Looking back now, I wish I hadn't done the ritual alone. It would have been different, more comforting and healing,

I think, if I could have shared the experience with others.

In my life, I did things that were harmful to myself, although I did not understand all the implications at the time. I criticized myself for being promiscuous and felt shame. Eventually, with help of Buddhist practices and therapy, I came to accept myself and did find a wonderful, loving man and married him. I still am learning how to receive kindness and also give it to myself. I think I am a sweet, loving person who empowers young women through work in the schools and a life of helping others. Although I have no children, I often work with children, teaching art projects and mentoring. Not every woman has to be a mother. I wasn't. There is an important place for aunts and teachers.

Alexa's Story

When Alexa was still in elementary school, she didn't know why, but she realized that her relationship with boys wasn't going in the same direction as others'. She couldn't see herself in the traditional model, married with a family and children. In her second year of college, Alexa fell in love with a woman. It was a few years later that she was able to release the guilt and shame she felt about her emerging orientation, as she realized that what she had inside of herself was wholesome, good and loving. She hoped for a long-term partner and children. This is Alexa's story.

Starting in my mid-twenties, I had a seven-year relationship with a wonderful woman who was an associate dean at a college in southern California. I had the sense that the relationship might continue over the long term, and we talked about having children together. After many years, I raised the question of whether she would be willing to have children with me even if we knew we weren't going to be together forever. She responded by telling me I needed to "shit or get off the pot" in the relationship. She was in love with me, loyal, and she would have stayed. Finally, at 32 years old, I made the difficult decision to leave.

In my mid-thirties, I had discussions with my best friend about what it would be like to be a single parent. I had been considering either adoption or artificial insemination. She assured me that she would be there for me and for my child. When I thought about adoption, the process seemed overwhelming and costly. In the back of my mind I began doubting whether or not I had the energy and money necessary to live as a single parent. I was very concerned about being poor.

Over the next few years I had a couple of different relationships and my biological clock was ticking. At 39 years old, I was in a relationship and had just entered the seminary; I felt the window for having a child was closing. I went to the doctor for a checkup and she said I was physically able to have a child. Around this time my partner moved out, while remaining a close friend. Again, I found myself to be single.

Regardless of my single relationship status and the related fear, I went to the sperm bank, selected a donor and got a tiny vial of sperm.

They send "the specimen" home with you in a tin that looks like an old milk can from a farm, with liquid nitrogen vapor to keep it frozen. My former partner and I did a ritual and she inseminated me. I had the feeling that it took. Later that day I went out and walked the dog, who jerked me all over the place, and I realized that it had probably been a dumb idea to take that walk. I did not become (or remain) pregnant, but I was not deterred.

Soon after that, I purchased more sperm, this time two vials at $200 per vial. I drove from California to Oregon with the vials—suspended in liquid nitrogen—strapped in a seatbelt in the passenger seat. My dear friend was a woman's health specialist and, the next day, we practiced with tubing and jelly in preparation to insert the sperm into my uterus. Needless to say, we laughed hysterically. Later that night, as we passed each other in the hallway going to bed, we locked eyes and shared a silent knowing that this process was going to work.

This was one of the most profound nights of my life. I couldn't fall asleep—I was wide awake for no apparent reason. At three o'clock, I got out of bed and went to the living room, trying to figure out why I wasn't sleeping. The message I received was that my body was doing everything it could to stop me from inseminating—that there was a fear in my body of getting pregnant. The "not sleeping" was a clear signal, and I got it. I decided not to inseminate. If I did, I felt it would be flirting with disaster. I went to bed and immediately fell asleep. In the morning we did a ritual while placing the sperm under a rose bush. It felt like burying a dream, returning the dream I had been carrying to the earth. That was the end of my dream of birthing a child. It was painful and sad. Though a difficult decision, I have never felt regret about my decision that night, nor wished that I had gone ahead.

I have come to realize that by settling for relationships that were not "always and forever"—not waiting for the right relationship—I now live with the consequence of not having a child. I made choices and I am doing a good job in the life that I created. But I do look back and wonder what would have happened if I had waited for "the one."

I remember back to my early twenties, when one of my friends urged me to at least experience sex with a man. Eventually I did—one time. I remember thinking afterward, *Oh my god, I could be pregnant,* and then wishing that it would happen. That would have been a turning point, a different trajectory for my life. I would have carried and birthed that child, but I don't know how I would have managed as a single mother.

My period came and I was disappointed. Pregnancy then would have been a portion of my dream fulfilled.

There is a piece of me that lives with the lingering loss, the loss of a dream. I never wanted anything more than a partner and a child and something interfered with my most compelling dream. Even now, a part of me believes that I might achieve that; that I might find a partner with children, that the dream could be fulfilled through an adopted family, not through birthing a child. At my age, being a grandparent is probably a more likely possibility.

My life is not what I hoped for or imagined; it's not my dream. But I have an incredible life doing wonderful things. I am a generative influence and creative part of my community. I experience satisfaction and joy in this expression as a professional minister and I feel good about that. I have also had some wonderful relationships with children of friends and family that have been very fulfilling.

Talking about these experiences and choices now leaves me with a mix of feelings. Sometimes I wonder if my life worked out better without the blessing and responsibility of children. Other times, I feel cheated that I haven't had the opportunity to parent. But one thing is clear: I am grateful for the life I have and know that I am blessed.

Betty's Story

Betty always expected to have children of her own. Her first marriage ended after four years, without producing any children. When she met her current husband, who is 13 years older than she is, he already had two children—a ten-year-old son and a 13-year-old daughter. Betty really wanted to have children, yet he didn't want to have any more so, when they were considering getting married, they went to therapy. Here's what Betty shared...s

There was a lot to consider. What if I didn't marry him and then still didn't have children? Or, what if I marry him, then get angry about being childless and we get divorced and it's too late for me to have children?

We were madly in love. He had wonderful children and was devoted to them and to me. I just couldn't imagine my future without this man. Realizing that I couldn't predict the future, it didn't feel right to make a decision based on what might or might not happen. So I agreed not to have children and we got married—he was 39 and I was 26.

Missing out on birthing and raising my own children, I was afraid my stepchildren would not love me like a mother. I also felt that my parents would be disappointed in me, especially as their only daughter.

A few years after we got married, when I was around 30 years old, I realized I was changing my mind and I felt guilty. We had an agreement, and this change of mind was betraying my husband. I shouldn't be changing my mind, but I couldn't put it out of my head. After sharing this with him, we went back to therapy. I think he felt bad about the dilemma and was nervous. We discussed various options, including adoption and artificial insemination, and both of us became very sad. He never changed his mind and, in retrospect, I'm thankful. He was true to himself. He did not want more children and it would never have worked. At the time, I was sad, resentful and angry about it. In one of the last sessions, the therapist said to me, "You are free to nurture and give all of your love to anyone, anywhere, anyway. You don't have to reserve any part of yourself because you will never run out of love."

I came out of that therapy realizing, *Maybe I'm not missing anything, maybe there isn't a huge hole here, maybe I can be happy without having my own children, maybe I can share that kind of love and relationship with my stepchildren.*

I felt it was my duty to society, the family and my parents to have children and I imagined others were critical of me for not having my own children. I felt they were thinking, "She's so self-centered." Pretending that all was well, I would explain, "We decided not to have children, but I have stepchildren." I was never pregnant and didn't even know if I could have ever conceived. I kept hoping the gynecologist would tell me that I couldn't have children—what a relief that would have been. Nothing to explain; nothing to feel ashamed or guilty about!

In my late twenties and early thirties, although I thought about babies daily, I never talked about my childlessness with my friends. I talked with my husband and the therapist. My family knew that my husband had a vasectomy, but we never talked about how they felt and how I felt. Later, my brother and sister-in-law invited me to be part of the birth of their third child. It was amazing. I felt so close to them and touched that they would invite me into that private part of their lives.

I loved being with babies, especially my nieces and nephews, and my husband and I spent a lot of time with them. But it wasn't like having my own. I felt sad and cried a lot until I reached 40. Then I realized it was too late. I began to understand my husband better, since he had been 39 when we got married.

We shared custody with my stepchildren's mother every other day, so there was cooperation and continuity in parenting. One thing I enjoyed about being a stepmother was the unique adult-child relationships that enabled us to talk about some things easier than they could with their own parents.

For a long time, I felt less than whole as a woman because I had no children, but not now. Over the years, I opened my heart and allowed myself to love them completely, and today they feel like my kids and I don't feel any sense of loss. In the past, when asked about children, I would explain I had stepchildren. Now I say "my daughter and son" or, at times, refer to myself as their "other mother."

In my forties, I went into a deep, dysfunctional, clinical depression and a few years later was diagnosed with breast cancer. I was so sick for those years and thanked God I didn't have young children because I wouldn't have been able to care for them. It would also have been a huge burden for my husband to have all that responsibility. Things have worked out. It wasn't always easy. At this point, I feel happy and fulfilled and am glad things have worked out so well.

Ten years ago, when my daughter was pregnant, I was so excited to become a grandmother. We talked a lot about what it was like for her and how it felt to carry a baby. She knew how significant that was for me.

Now I have four grandchildren who call me Grammy. It is such a joy to be on an equal basis with their other grandparents. I adore the temporary responsibility of nurturing and caring for them. No one questions my being a grandmother. I feel more authentic. I belong.

I missed out on the experience of carrying life inside my body, but it's okay. It's been helpful for me to talk about this with you and be heard.

Stella's Story

At 15, Stella knew that she would never marry. She could never imagine having children. As a child, her house was hell and there was no way she would ever reproduce that. She made that vow to herself because she felt that marriage and children were the wrong things for her to do. Here is Stella's story.

Pregnancy didn't appeal to me, there was never the appropriate partner and there were already too many people in the world. My image was never as a mother, more as a caretaker. There is little understanding or honoring of the choice not to want children. At times, when people are engrossed with their families, I don't fit in. Nevertheless, I am happy with my choices.

Parenting is an honorable thing to do—an enormous task that I greatly respect. An awakening that was extremely helpful for me in seeing certain of my talents and abilities was becoming a chiropractor. In everything I do, I have a fine attention and presence and the quality of going inside. I came to realize how much I had to give to children and the expression of my creativity is how that need has been met. Slowly, in my forties, I had come to realize that my character is very solid.

I used to love spending time with my young nieces and they always commented on how much fun I was. After a career as a chiropractor, I became an elementary school teacher. I knew that, as a teacher, the children would love me, but I didn't know if they would get on my nerves. Over the years, I have had many great experiences as a teacher, but I was continually surprised to learn how lenient many parents were. In this society, there didn't seem to be such a thing as right and wrong or honoring of elders. There was permissiveness without clear boundaries, and lack of responsibility. It was confusing. Earlier in my life, traveling in Africa and Mexico, I found the children much better behaved than the average child in my classroom. I have felt like a "fuddy-duddy" at times; an obsolete lion.

Although I have a strong sense of my own mythology—who I am as a soul—I feel completely misplaced almost everywhere in society.

It seems that the way people belong and create their identity in our culture is to have children. I am a woman from a Holocaust family, without my own tribe. I could have been an "auntie" in a village. But, without that village, I have endured years of pain, with no family of my own, trying to become part of others' families. Who do I have to teach how to cook, how to sew, to share my sense of awe in being alive?

Over the years I have had to defend my choices—never married, no children—as if there was something wrong with me. My sister said I should tell people I had been married before, even though I wasn't. That wasn't honest and it wasn't me. It is accepted to have children, even outside of marriage, but not so acceptable to choose to have no child at all.

As a teacher, there was one time when I did consider adopting one of the children in my class who had a mother on crack cocaine. I would have been good for him. He really needed a mother. He had a lot in him and he needed to have someone who loved him. It would have been a lot of trouble for me and I didn't know if I wanted to give that much of myself up.

Now in my sixties, I sometimes think it was a mistake not having my own children. I definitely did not want to do it on my own. I think if I'd met a man who really wanted children, I would have had kids. Being a parent is holy. The teachings are enormous and the gifts are enormous. I probably would have been a wonderful mother. I would have had a lot of presence, as did my mother. Sometimes I think I missed out on a certain depth and continuity of relationship. I'm a very deep person and I think it would have been a powerful experience for me. However, I'm also not tortured by something that could have been torture to me. You never know how it would have worked out.

I treasure my inner life—I have had time for that. I was very close to my own mother, and I am close to my niece. I would have liked acknowledgment that, as an unmarried woman with no children, I was honored and belonged. In a tribal culture, there is a place for a person like me, perhaps as a shaman. There is an initiation into a pathway, it is a belonging: "This person chose not to marry. They are using their energy in a different way that is important." I would have appreciated being acknowledged for taking on a different level of beingness, which is valuable.

I was never a mother. I had no internal driving force to have children, or else I would have had them. It might have been nice to be a grandmother. I do have animals and I love my animals. If I had to live without animals or without color, I don't think I could do it. I can live without children.

Jasmine's Story

Until Jasmine was pregnant the first time, she had not thought much about having children. She wasn't one of the girls who dreamt about it or planned for it. That all changed when she became pregnant. As Jasmine was growing up, she imagined love and a relationship as she saw her life unfolding. It wasn't until her mid-thirties that Jasmine connected with her desire to have a child. This is her story.

After spending all of my twenties working on myself, being in a few long-term relationships, traveling, going to school and being part of a spiritual community, I met my husband. We married when I was 32. Even after marriage, having children wasn't a question we were trying to answer—it was about the love between us.

A few years into our marriage, something changed. One day we both woke up and said, "We should have a baby." That's where we were in life and it felt right to both of us. When my next period didn't arrive, I took a pregnancy test and we were pregnant. Everything in me changed.

Earlier, the way I was living my life felt like it was exactly how it was meant to be. Now pregnant, it felt the right thing at the right moment. There was no stress. It felt natural and easy. We were thrilled. My husband would have been fine with or without children, but if we were going to have children, he said he would like five of them. All of a sudden, my whole life was different and we were making space for a baby. How happy I was about that was shocking to me—surprising and beautiful.

Far away from home at 12 weeks and sensing there was something wrong, I went to the emergency room and learned there was no heartbeat. I was totally unprepared and devastated. This was the most horrible experience of my life. Choosing to let the miscarriage proceed naturally rather than have a D&C, I left the ER, but, by the next day, I was seriously hemorrhaging and had to be admitted to the hospital. I felt deep grief at the loss and found myself crying endlessly. My husband flew out to be with me and somehow the time we had together during all of this bonded us very deeply. We came through it with deep love and compassion, together. The level of sorrow and hurt during this time was immense. I was now deeply connected to the desire to be a mother, and the grief seemed unending.

My doctor was encouraging, telling me that a miscarriage was not unusual. Soon I was pregnant again and, while aware, I was not concerned about having another miscarriage. But, at 12 weeks, I miscarried again. This time I chose a D&C and still went through all the emotional turmoil of the loss.

Afraid there was something wrong with me, I thought we should do tests. The doctor disagreed, until my third pregnancy also ended in miscarriage at 12 weeks. It was found that I have a "Protein S Deficiency," which causes miscarriages at 12 weeks. It was also determined that I could take a drug that increases the chances of carrying a pregnancy by 50 percent, but the drug has other, serious side effects.

I had to step back and ask, *What is my body telling me? What is modern medicine telling me? How much do I want to exert my will? Do I want a baby so much that I am willing to risk my health and another miscarriage?* It took me about a year to come to a decision. This process became a deeply spiritual questioning—my will or surrender to what life is giving me? I needed to ask myself, *Why do I want a baby? For me? Do I think it will make me whole? Or happy? Or fulfilled?* This was difficult. Everyone around me was having babies and joining the "Mommy Club" and nobody seemed to be asking the questions I had to ask. Through this quest, I came to the decision not to get pregnant again.

And so began the emotional process around "not being a mom." I could not have predicted how, over the next ten years, I went through such grief and deep emotion. Not having kids was a difficult decision; perhaps equally as hard has been moving toward 50 and living with that choice.

As life unfolded, my husband and I ended our marriage. Not too long after that, I met the man I'm now married to. I also married his three beautiful young daughters and began the journey of being a stepmom. The first six months of our relationship involved all five of us and was bonding and blissful. It all seemed so simple. The girls were very much in favor of the relationship. It seemed like it couldn't be any better and I felt blessed. We share custody equally with their birth mother, who has been in a long-term relationship from before the time I met their father.

I love the girls and they love me, but it's clear to me every day: I'm not their mother. Surprisingly, the deepest grief and loss I've experienced of not being a mother has come from being a stepmother. Somehow, as a stepparent, I am an outsider. I can be there for them with my whole heart and still not be the person they want. It is so painful when they come running into my arms hugging me and crying, "I want my mommy." I couldn't have imagined what that statement would touch in me—being so close to a child, but not being the "right" one.

The challenges I face with the mother of my three stepdaughters are typical for stepfamilies. I think having another woman in the girls' lives is just really hard for their mom, and that in turn makes it difficult for the girls. And for me, I can be deeply committed to them, present in every way, but without permission from their birth mother, it's very challenging. I look like a mother and operate like a mother, but I'm not the mother.

My relationship with the girls is as good as it gets, but the birth parent-child relationship is primary. Sometimes I think it would be easier and less painful not to have children than to be a stepmother. I do my best to have a sense of humor. Otherwise, I can get pretty tortured over it all.

Over the years I have come to understand what it means to be a mother, and yet not a mother. It has been a spiritual journey for me, coming to understand where I belong in the world. With no birth children, I sometimes have a sense of floating. Motherhood gives women a sense of identity so we don't have to answer the question of who we are in this world. *Who will want my treasures when I die?* The self-reflection that I have experienced has brought me compassion. I have needed to find other places in myself, places of inner strength and connection.

I treasure my friends without children. In the spiritual community, and in my work, there are a lot of women living childfree, and I always saw it as an option. Now, one of my close friends in her forties is desperate to have a baby. That driving force is not in me. I have to ask, *Who is this baby for? Why do I want this?* As women, I think we need to be willing to ask those questions.

As the years have unfolded, I've moved from feeling like a "victim" of what happened to owning *This is my life.* It was an important transition for me when I went from saying, "I couldn't have children," to, "Having children is not my path in this life." I have great respect for what life has to offer me. My life doesn't fit into the traditional trajectories; however, it is meaningful and I don't have regrets. In this lifetime, having my own children hasn't been my path.

Emily's Story

At 19, Emily was in love and had been living with her boyfriend for a year when she found herself pregnant. She told her boyfriend. His reaction made her realize that he was not in love with her. He said, "I can't marry you because we have already had sex and that is against my religion, and I don't believe in abortion, but I want you to have an abortion." Emily was shocked by his response and that he didn't even consider talking about it. She had always wanted to have a big family and she wanted to have this baby, but was afraid to do it alone. Her boyfriend just wanted her to disappear. Disappointed and numb, she drove back to her hometown and had an abortion. Here is the rest of Emily's story.

Later, in two other relationships, while using birth control, I became pregnant and, each time, felt a great deal of shame that it had happened. Besides the men involved, who didn't want the child, I can't remember telling anyone. I was scared to make the decision to have a child on my own, for the sake of the child who would not have a stable environment and for my own inability to get it together. I didn't trust myself. I always wanted children, but I never found the partner who was choosing me and saying, "Let's do this, let's create a family."

Two years into a relationship with a lovely, free-spirited man who loved me, but clearly never wanted to be a father, and after three abortions, I conceived once again, at 32 years old. Just about the time I realized that I was pregnant—about 25 days along—my beloved older stepsister and her husband stopped for a visit on their way home from two months in China. She was 13 years older and had always been close and supportive of me. During the visit, she and I were sitting next to a waterfall on a rock with our arms around each other and she shared with me that she and her husband had now decided to adopt a child, probably from China, since scarring from an illegal abortion when she was a teenager had made it impossible for her ever to be pregnant. I looked at her and said, "I think I know why you are here right now," and then told her I thought I was pregnant and my partner didn't want to be a father. She said, "We would love to adopt your child." The two of us made a pact right there. Later, in the same sentence that I told my partner that I was pregnant, I also shared with him that my sister and her husband were going to adopt the child. It was settled.

I got to say "yes" to having a child, but it was bittersweet. I was already in love with her and I knew that, adopted, she would have everything. I felt I was taking the best care of my child. During the pregnancy, I talked to her and explained how much I loved her, and cried with her, and told her why I made the decision I did. There were many omens throughout the pregnancy that supported my decision and I was totally committed.

The birth was amazing. All four parents were there and the photograph of the waterfall was projected onto the wall over the hot tub where my daughter was born. I stayed and nursed her for six weeks. Leaving her was so difficult, but I knew it was my time to exit.

Back home, I cried and cried and cried. In support of my healing, my best friend encouraged me to try on the thought of how it would be if I changed my mind: "I'm here to take my child back." In doing that, I realized the pain would just shift from me to my sister and I knew then that I could live with the pain. That really helped me live with my decision. Part of our agreement was that they would send money for two years so I could visit every six months.

I was an aunt now, although my sister always told the child that she had come from my belly, not her mother's belly. Those visits with her, when I was with her all day as her parents worked, built my confidence that I could be a mother, where previously I had been unsure. I had been so fearful of recreating my mother's life. I have visited my daughter every year since she was born. She is now 16.

From then on, I made changes in my life to allow me to have a child. Cleaning up any loose strings from the past—making apologies and amends—but still no partner.

Having studied Buddhism for years, I traveled to Thailand and Nepal. Everywhere I went they asked, "Where is your husband? Where are your children? What is wrong with you?" Unexpectedly, I met the man who would become my husband and we were married in Kathmandu. Now I could have children. Back in the U.S., a year after we were married, I became pregnant. My husband was supportive, although I don't know if he really wanted a child or was even in love with me. He came from a culture where marriages are arranged and the expectations are different. I loved being pregnant. I was delighted. I felt supported, in a protective bubble, and was constantly talking with the child. The relationship between my husband and me was challenging because of the cultural differences. He had never had to work and expected me to take care of him as his mother had. I felt burdened and alone and desperately needed space to take care of myself, so we separated for a while.

For the last couple of months of the pregnancy, my husband and I were living in a beautiful place where I gave birth to our son. I felt elated. It was a glorious, easy time. It all felt perfect. Things fell into place in our family life for a while. Then, two years later, we separated again and, a number of years after that, he asked for a divorce. By then I had my own house and my own life and it was just some paperwork to sign. Over the years, he has been present as a father and it is easy between us. Our son is 11 years old.

This summer, my sister, her husband and daughter came for a visit, as did her birth father. We were all in the house together with my son. It was the first time in my niece's memory that she had spent time with her father and I think she came to understand who he was and why he couldn't father her. Everything was open and honest and joyous.

I feel I made the right decisions, even about the abortions. I never have created the family I had hoped for, but I am a great parent. My intention is there. I pay attention. It's what I've always wanted. When I was younger, I wasn't prepared to be a parent. I didn't have the skills or the confidence. I'm grateful that I had choice.

Sarah's Story

Sarah's family had just moved from a small town in the east to a city in the west as a result of her father's affairs. Both of her working class parents were functional alcoholics and all five of them—her parents, brother, sister and herself—were living in an efficiency apartment. It was a trying time. Sarah felt displaced. Even though she was at the edge of leaving the nest, she felt that she needed to stay with the family since she was worried about leaving her 12-year-old sister alone there. As the oldest, Sarah had always been the helper. She was barely 19 and there was no money for her to go to school, barely money to eat. Sarah shares her story...

I was new to the city and casually dating a local truck driver who was about ten years older when kissing turned into forced date rape. I was scared, said "No" many times and cried all the way through it. After it was over, I said to him, "I'm afraid I'll get pregnant." With a smile on his face, he said, "Then I'll have you just where I want you." I was terrified. My heart shut down. I felt he had done it on purpose and hoped I was pregnant, that he could imprison me for life. I never saw him again, although he pursued me. I totally shut him out. My usually regular period did not come. I waited two weeks before I told my parents. They really showed up for me. My mother did say, "Too bad you don't love him." But, when I replied, "No, I don't love him, he scares me," she heard me.

There was no way I was willing to be connected to that man in any way and I don't think he ever knew I was pregnant. I was terrified at the thought of becoming a single welfare mother scraping along for decades. My working parents had barely been able to support our family, so I had experienced that growing up. I wanted a different life for myself and for any child I might have. I was not ready to be a mother, I still felt like a child myself.

My mother worked hard to find out what we could do to end the pregnancy. It was before *Roe v. Wade*. She found a psychiatrist that I could talk with who then had to present my case to a panel of doctors to get approval for a therapeutic abortion. I cried with relief when I got the "yes" from the psychiatrist.

Throughout the pregnancy, I regularly spoke to the baby within me, telling it that I could not carry it, that I was so sorry for what I had to do. I was terrified of becoming a welfare mom and didn't know if I would have ever recovered from birthing a child and then having to give the child up for adoption. I knew I had to terminate the pregnancy. Thankfully, my parents fully supported my decision and even paid for the procedure.

Because it had taken so long to get permission, the pregnancy had progressed beyond 12 weeks and the abortion was done by injecting saline solution into my uterus with a long needle through my abdomen. I had to stay in the hospital and the cramping started in the middle of the night when I was alone in the dark. They had placed a large mat under me to catch the bloody mess. After it was over, the nurse came to roll up the mat and take it away, still in the dark. She said to me in a way that sounded shaming, "Look what you have done." I replied, "I know what I have done." I didn't feel shame. I felt grief and relief, but no shame. I knew it was better for all of us—for me, the child, my family, the future—than the alternative. Any other way was way too hard. This was the only choice.

I know my mother loved me. I was the first child. My parents were 20 years old and married childhood sweethearts. They wanted me. But as time went on, my mother became jealous of the relationship that developed between my father and me. I was his "number one," his "sweet pea," and all his attention went to me, especially when they were having difficulty relating. I loved the attention. My brother was born three years later and wasn't wanted, as I had been. Later, my sister was born. My mother had a victim streak and was submissive to my father. Both of them drank. I didn't want to repeat that.

When I was a child, I had a spirit guide. She wore a blue velvet cape with a hood—almost Celtic. She helped me understand that the craziness in my parents was from alcohol, that I had to protect my siblings.

When I was 20 years old, I married a Marine. It was my way out of the house, but it was hard leaving my little sister unprotected. Being married was like we were playing house—we had a good time and I felt safe. He never wanted to have children and I was on the pill. When he left the Marine Corps three years later, he wanted his freedom. We separated and eventually got a divorce.

Although I always tried to prevent further pregnancies, I had two more before I was 25 years old. In one, the IUD slipped in my uterus, and the other was the result of a broken condom. Both of the abortions were performed in a clinic with supportive medical staff. There was no judgment. Although I had a lot of tears, I was not alone. I was terrified of being a single mother and neither of the men would have been appropriate partners or parents. If I had found a partner who wanted to be a parent and would be a good one, then I would have had children.

Now in my sixties, I have been pondering life and death and impermanence and being in the moment—all those thread together in the fabric of my thoughts. I found a Rumi poem:

> *When my pain became the cause of my cure*
> *My contempt changed into reverence*
> *And my doubt into certainty.*
> *I see that I have been the veil on my path.*
> *Now my body has become my heart*
> *My heart has become my soul*
> *And my spirit, the eternal Spirit.*

It triggered all sorts of thoughts about my life, things that I regretted, going through grief, feeling it completely and letting it have its way, but not acting out or grabbing on. Getting at the truth of my responsibility about what happened. Taking responsibility and forgiving myself.

I am sad I had to abort the babies. I think about how old they would be now and how I could have managed. At 19, I couldn't do it. I know it was the best choice. I love babies and children, I love being with them. I have a connection with kids and with old people. When I was approaching 40 years old, I knew I had to choose that I wasn't ever going to be a mother. I don't regret not having children. I regret having to end the pregnancies—preventing something from growing into its full potential.

I spend a lot of time alone. I have no close family. I wonder who will care for me if I can't. My younger sister struggles to keep her own life stable and organized. She had two children as a single mother. She lived what I was afraid to live and is still suffering at 50 years old. She would care for me, but it would be very difficult. My brother, though kindhearted, is a basket case—the town drunk.

I have specific points in my life where I can remember standing at a crossroads, realizing there were a number of directions I could have gone and they all led to some place very different. Which one? You just have to take one and go for it before you can even get a glimpse of where it will take you. You never know where the other ones would have taken you.

I feel really grateful. I have had a good life filled with grace. I was graced that I was the firstborn and got the best parenting from my parents, when they were young and in love, which was gone later. At times, I feel guilty because I got all their love as a young child.

As an adult, I have had amazing adventures. I traveled many places in the world. I made a choice early on that I wasn't going to do the dedicated career path. I would be present to opportunities. I even lost all my money in a Ponzi scheme. I am amazed at how resilient I am. I am a natural entrepreneur, have created a number of businesses and had a good time doing it. I have learned a lot. I've lived my life. I know the difference between alone and lonely. I've learned so much about myself. I can know what I want, what is nurturing for me, and finally I trust myself. I feel good about my life.

Talking about these experiences with you now has been valuable— having a place to speak and be heard, having someone who really listens, not just running it around in my own mind.

Barbara's Story

There are no children in my house. No kids come home for the holidays. No child resents me for the bad job of loving that they think I did. All I know of mother-love, I know from observation and my experience as a child on the receiving end of the fierce and somewhat devouring love of my mother. I do not know what it feels like to love a child with ferocity. Nor do I know whether my mother-love would have been fierce, perhaps it would have been painfully and joyously tender.

It might be assumed either that I had no choice or that I made a choice not to have children. Rather, for many years, I made the choice to put off the decision and never made the choice to have a child. I felt like a child for far too long and too late to fit a child in before conditions were no longer supportive.

I did conceive when I was 41. I had an abortion. It was sad. I think it was right. I do not know. That was many years ago now. The thing that makes me sad is that I know I would have loved my child. I know that I would sit here with another love gripping me. I know I would have taken care of my child. My own sense of responsibility, a particular form, which demanded that I take of care of everything and everyone before myself, made the thought of a child's demands overwhelming. And my partner didn't want a child, so I would have been alone.

I had assumed I would be a mother at some point in my life. When I was young, I loved acting and everything about the theater; that is, everything except how it might intrude on that other passion of my life—being loved by another person. Since I thought I wanted family, and since acting seemed impractical, I decided not to pursue theater. It would take me away from family. My family was abstract at this point, mainly consisting of a man who loved me. It was a cozy place.

I have led a peripatetic life and have no children. I don't spend a lot of time in regret; however, when my friend asked what was the one thing I did regret, I did not hesitate in answering: "I regret not pursuing acting." I did not say I regret the absence of a son or daughter, though I sometimes imagine it would have been deeply engaging. However, the absence of children feels almost right *and* sad at the same time. Giving up on theater in my late teens seems like a betrayal of my passion.

When I was 21 (in the late Sixties), I met Rick and fell in love. From fairly early on we would talk about growing old together, but we didn't talk about children. We did at times worry about pregnancy, as in, "I hope I'm not pregnant." I thought that marriage was not important and was somewhat *common*, which I did not want to be. It was fine to have a child as a single parent, but children were a huge responsibility and I did not want to take that on alone. Our relationship wasn't stable. We broke up, became friends, toyed with the idea of getting back together, continued our relationship long distance until Rick asked me to marry him and live in Nepal on his Fulbright grant.

I had a hard time reconciling my deep desire to marry Rick with my fears about marriage and my fears about Rick, as well as my ideas about life and what *should* matter. In considering my decision, I never included children. I felt that neither of us was ready to consider such a thing. My desire, accompanied by love and a mysterious and deep connection, won, and Rick and I married. I was somewhat embarrassed about getting married and was relieved when my friends were supportive.

During the years we lived in Nepal, I assumed that having a child was not a consideration. Rick was supported by a grant just adequate for our needs and was very committed to the research he was doing. With a new MFA in sculpture and textiles, I was not very good at generating money and really wanted to make art.

One afternoon, Rick and I made a potential baby. I remember knowing I had become pregnant. I did not want to be pregnant and I did not think Rick wanted me to be pregnant. I remember telling him I was worried. I thought about how I could go to Bangkok and get an abortion. I worried about money—we had very little. Rick wouldn't want anything to get in the way of his research and I assumed he would consider a baby in the way. I couldn't imagine being a mother under these conditions. My period was late. I waited. Then my period started. It was very light and continued for two or three days. I was relieved that I was not pregnant. One night, about eight weeks after conceiving, I started to bleed. The next day I arranged to go to the doctor. Rick asked me if I wanted him to come along. He had previously scheduled to do something for his research and I didn't want to intrude on his schedule so I said, "No, I'll be fine on my own." I thought bravado was required. I regret that decision.

I ran errands in the morning, mapping my course so I would have access to a fairly clean bathroom every 20 minutes or so. That afternoon at the clinic it was confirmed I had been pregnant. I completed my miscarriage with the "C" of the D&C. No dilation was required. I held the hand of a female German doctor who was thereafter my friend.

I was fascinated by the experience and embarrassed and confused and sad. It felt private, like mine alone. I had never been recognized as pregnant, so I had not lost anything. I had worried that I was pregnant and was certain that I could not, would not, have a child at this time. Assuming that Rick did not want a child, I didn't trouble him with thinking or talking about the possibility or what to do. I always gave the impression that I was very clear on this and that we didn't need to dwell on it unless I was pregnant for sure. When I thought I had gotten my period, that was that, though I was still uncertain about the state of my uterus.

Looking back, I think it is strange how little we spoke about pregnancy and children—a leftover from our twenties, when we were unmarried and uncertain about commitment. A pregnancy would have been very unfortunate then. But, in our thirties, it might have been a consideration. I think we tried to read each other's minds concerning children more than in any other area of life. I remember one time when Rick cried after a movie that included a playful father and son. We were still in Nepal. He was about 33 and afraid he would never have that relationship. I was surprised and scared by his reaction. I was also touched. As it turned out, years later (a year or so after we split up), Rick did marry his pregnant girlfriend and fell madly in love with his son. He loved being a father.

Rick was very kind to me after the miscarriage. I was stunned and tired. I had learned I had become pregnant and then lost the abstractly unwanted pregnancy all in one day. I had also had a D&C without much of any anesthesia. I figured I should just get over it and turned it into an interesting story. I wasn't devastated. I was fascinated. I found myself needing to know how large the fetus was. A magazine article in the doctor's office had photographs of developmental stages of a fetus. I wanted to know everything. I didn't talk to anyone about this fascination, or, if I did, it was in a very abstract manner, turning it into an intellectual curiosity rather than a compelling human experience.

That pea-sized fetus was mine, made from me and Rick, and I had never even said "hello" before it was gone. And I never really said "goodbye" either. It was a clinical event with confusing undertones. I knew something had happened. I wasn't quite sure what. Few others knew about it, and I didn't talk about my feelings much, as I recall.

Was my *choice* not to have children sensible? Given my risky creative urges, I think it probably was. Was it made in a way that honored my life, my capacities, my senses, my urges? I think not. The women's movement surged when I was in college, providing women with greater choice. That made it easy for me to think about choosing not to have children and avoid recognizing the repercussions of that choice. I thought I had forever. If I could choose not to have a child, I could later choose to have a child.

In my forties, when I again became pregnant, I was in a fairly new relationship. On the rational level, I pretty much knew I would have an abortion. However, after my experience in Nepal with the miscarriage, I wanted to give myself time to settle with my decision. I also kept suspecting that I would miscarry. This time I wouldn't be alone. My sister and boyfriend came to the hospital with me and, a few days later, a friend led me in a ritual, drumming and singing and speaking to the little spirit. It felt good to honor the spirit of the fetus, to send it on its way, to do my best to set it free. I felt that I had done the right thing to end the pregnancy. The ritual was important to me and seemed right, even if I had felt a bit foolish doing it.

The other day, I was talking to my current husband about this whole area of a woman's life. I was saying how useful it would be for younger women of childbearing age to have some venue for seriously investigating the options of choosing childlessness or motherhood. I started to say, "I wish I had had someone to talk to about this," and I found myself sobbing. I realized how much I would have welcomed an open space to investigate my own feelings and potential choices and the meaning of those choices. It seems to me that my loss has been that I did not have a place and the inner structure to explore the choice with tenderness—tenderness for myself, my partner or women who make other choices. It is the bravado that hurts—the pretense that I thought I knew what I was doing, the need to be cool, hip, above all the "silly feminine stuff," above gender roles and so on. My tears make the point—this arena of a woman's life is deep and poorly attended; nature, society, family all create unspoken urges and expectations. How can we know and attend to what we hardly recognize or speak of?

I believe that I made my choice in defiance of the status quo and supported by a movement that was in a rather defiant stage. I missed the opportunity to hang out with the losses inherent in the choice and so I needed bravado and defiance to hold me up. It is not that I believe I would have chosen to have a child, but that my choice not to have a child could have been held with tenderness rather than bravado.

Choice includes loss. I think it is best to investigate and feel it out, to make the choice, to acknowledge and grieve the loss. And no one should have to grieve in isolation.

I do not regret not having children. Sometimes I feel like I've missed out on something. But this does not differ in degree from thinking that I missed out by not traveling alone overseas in my twenties or that I didn't understand about buying a house until I was in my forties.

Friends with children tell me that, once they had a child, they felt an immediate connection with all other mothers. Regardless of economic status or race or culture, connection was established. I had friends who were desperate to be mothers. Though I was a supportive friend, I was puzzled by their desperation. I have never longed for a child. I have been interested in experiencing many things in my life. Motherhood seemed like an infringement on my opportunities, that I could not be a mother *and* everything else I wanted to be. Certainly my mother gave me the sense that she gave up a lot for her children. My focus in life has been creativity, but in a different venue than my womb.

Part Three

GRIEVING, HEALING
AND CLAIMING WHOLENESS

*We need a cultural shift that recognizes the vast number of women who experience **missed motherhood** and then teaches us—individually, with each other, as a community, as a society—how to support them. The loss of **missed motherhood** doesn't disappear, but the grief can, and our experience of the loss can shift. When that happens, we open space to become fully present to opportunities that are available to us in our lives.*

Recognizing Losses and Choices

"To become whole means that as we open to the pain, we open to the loss. We break open and, as a consequence, we get bigger and include more in life."
— DEBORAH MORRIS CORYELL, *Good Grief,*
Healing Through the Shadow of Loss

For most of us, life has not unfolded the way we expected it to—in many respects, it may be better; in others, worse. But, for just about every one of us, it's different than what we thought it would be. Beginning in our childhood, we create dreams of what our life as an adult will be, or what we would like it to be, or what it should be. Especially for little girls, children are commonly a part of that dream—we want them, or we don't want them, or we have a question about it.

Many women who want children fulfill that dream but then the decades-long experience of being a mother isn't what they imagined—it's better or worse or both, but almost certainly different. They may even have had unexpected and unshared experiences of *missed motherhood* along the way. If they didn't know how to process the loss incurred through these experiences, maybe they just "moved on," perhaps they had another child, all without fully grieving and healing. The grief may lie buried and hidden within, resurfacing in surprising ways. Or it may be a secret sorrow that quietly, unknowingly, saps energy and restrains their ability to be fully alive.

Other women, who fully expected to be mothers, may have found that it never happened for them—perhaps they never had the right partner, or they had a partner who didn't want children, or they could never conceive or birth a child, or their career was too demanding, or they waited too long to decide. Often, they blame themselves—*If only I'd done it differently*—feel shame, guilt or both.

Remember the fairy tales from our childhoods? We find our Prince Charming—or, preferably, he finds us—and we get married and live happily ever after, also with the assumption that we will have children and create a family. As girls, we have our dolls to play with as practice for motherhood. Often they are dolls of our choosing and we get to be in total control of when we play with them, how we dress them, what we do with them and the stories we create about them. All of those childhood experiences created unconscious and conscious beliefs in us about life and our ability to control our destiny. The fairy tales and the practicing felt real and predicted our future.

No one told us that the vast majority of women would experience *missed motherhood* and that many women would experience it more than once. Rather, it appeared to be an aberration, occurring in only a tiny number of women. When it happened to us, it meant we were flawed. The message we got was that it was better not to talk about it; better to keep it hidden and put on a brave face. No wonder we don't know how to deal with the loss and grief and pain! Talking about it was not sanctioned or supported, so how could we learn?

Women who *chose* not to have children—to live childfree—probably made that decision because they believed the gains outweighed any losses for them. Later in life, having experienced the full impact of their decision, many of these women become more aware of what the subsequent downsides, as well as the benefits have been for them. Not that they regret their choice. Most, with full awareness, would choose it again. Others are not so certain.

As women, our choices used to be a lot more limited. Society set the standards and, if we wanted to belong, we followed them. As women's rights and options have expanded, so have the choices we have to make. It's not as simple and clear-cut as it was before. More choice also requires letting go of options we do not choose, possibly incurring loss.

Our culture is not skilled at dealing with loss. We are supposed to be winners, not losers. Anything perceived as losing is often held as shameful. As a consequence, talking about losses is generally avoided, whether it's about money, a job, a relationship, a pregnancy, infertility or the possibility of having a child. We suffer in silence. It seems the acceptable way to act.

In our family, our mother didn't tell us until we were adults that she had had a miscarriage after our older brother was born. It was the day of her mother's funeral. She told us that she had hemorrhaged so massively that the doctors didn't think they could save her life. During the crisis, she floated out of her body in what she much later learned was a near-death experience. When she shared this information with her minister, he told her never to tell anyone because they would think she was crazy. She never did until she was in her seventies.

Although death is a part of life, in our culture it seems like it is to be denied at all costs, no matter the circumstances. To push back the inevitable, people are willing to pay astronomical amounts in hopes of staying alive just one more day or month. Even doctors often consider the death of a patient—no matter how old or terminally ill—as a failure. When someone dies, it becomes public knowledge. Even though we may feel awkward, not knowing how much of our sadness we can express or how to support others who are grieving, we can go to the funeral.

Missed motherhood is a loss that is unseen by others unless we bring it to their attention. It is difficult to know how to share about a miscarriage or an abortion if people didn't even know we were pregnant. Also, when hearing this news from another woman, we can wonder how to respond. What if pregnancy loss happens for a woman more than once? Or, struggling with trying to become pregnant, how can a woman share her feelings as, each month, it doesn't happen? How many times is too many times to talk about it?

Some cultures view loss differently, less tragically, more incorporated into the flow of life. They have rituals to honor losses and transitions; rituals that bring knowledge of them into the community experience, that support and join in the grieving, that encourage the expression of a range of feelings and open the space to release sorrow and move forward in life. One example of this is the *Mizuko-kuyo* ceremony, held at temples in Japan. During these ceremonies, women can honor the loss of a pregnancy from miscarriage, abortion or stillbirth with a memorial *Jizo* statue and attendance at a monthly memorial service.

In an attempt to soothe a woman who is experiencing *missed motherhood*, there are phrases that may slip off our tongues that actually encourage hiding and feelings of isolation, rather than providing support or an expression of healing. If you experienced *missed motherhood* yourself, you might have heard them; you might have even uttered them to your friends or family about their loss: "Time heals." "You'll get over it." "Get busy and have another baby." "It's probably for the best." "You already have a child/children." "It wasn't meant to be."

Then there are the things we tell ourselves—quietly, secretly, within our own minds—and hold to be the truth. I can remember some of mine: *My life is ruined. Nothing else matters now. I can never get over this. There is something wrong with me. I am flawed, less than a woman, not really feminine. No man would really want me. I don't fit in. I don't belong.* Another common one I've heard is: *I'm being punished by God.*

Without really being aware, many of us believe that life will happen according to our dreams, expectations and intentions. It has been said, "If you want to make God laugh, just tell Him your plans." Or, as John Lennon wrote, "Life is what happens to you while you're busy making other plans." Nowadays, many of us are being told that we are in control of our life and our future. It's up to us. If we are clear about our intentions, then the universe will deliver; if it doesn't, then it is our fault. When things don't happen the way we want, then these beliefs can lead to guilt and shame and more hiding.

Some believe that we are spiritual beings having human experiences and that our time on Earth is an opportunity to experience life as a human being, which includes loss and grief and learning. Free will allows us to make choices about how to deal with the challenges that life brings us. We don't know if it's true, but it is a frame that may help put life's challenges and losses in perspective.

There are so many choices that we make in life, big and small. Lots of choices made even in the course of a day. Each decision point includes the possibilities of gaining and losing. If I choose eggs for breakfast, I lose the opportunity for waffles that day. When I choose the college I will attend, I lose the opportunity to attend the others. When we like the choice we are making, it is easier to let the other possibilities go, even though we are losing them. Yes, they are lost opportunities, but we like the one we chose better. That's the way it is, unless we find that the choice we made didn't turn out the way we thought it would. Then we wonder if we made a mistake: *I married the wrong man*, or *I'm in the wrong job*, or *This house I just bought has mold in the walls.* At that point, it is easy to experience regret, even to feel a victim of our own choice and come to doubt ourselves.

There is an interesting research study about decision-making that was conducted by Daniel Gilbert, Ph.D., and his colleagues. They discovered, first of all, that almost all decisions are based on our predictions of the emotional consequences of our actions. Secondly, they found out that "when it comes to predicting exactly how you will feel in the future, you are most likely wrong," and that our mistaken expectations can lead directly to mistakes in our choices. It is reassuring to learn that they also found that we're happier with closure, one way or another, and less pleased when we have time to change our minds than when our choice is irrevocable. The freedom that finality brings in dealing with *missed motherhood* was recognized by a number of the women I spoke with, as well as myself.

Choice and loss are interconnected, each part of the whole. When we become afraid of loss, don't know how to process it, try to avoid it at all costs, it can paralyze us. We can get lost in pain with no way to process it and feel rage at the world. We find this situation in many of our clients, especially when it is critical for their self-image to get it right, to be perfect. Then any loss can be catastrophic, unendurable. Shame that there is something wrong with us, or guilt that we have done something wrong, can keep us in hiding. Secrecy, suppression, denial can seem the only way to survive or move on. But it doesn't work that way.

Unacknowledged and unshared feelings create isolation and separation. In fact, when there is no place to acknowledge our losses and process the pain, we may become obsessed with them and allow loss and pain to define and limit us. In reaction to the lack of recognition by others, our mind can become compelled to hold onto the loss—and its dimensions can even expand—in an unconscious attempt to validate its existence and meaning in our lives. If we don't remember, it would be like it never happened, yet it did. Or, if it is too painful, we may repress the memory, push it down into seeming oblivion, even though it is still claiming our energy.

Loss needs to be acknowledged, honored and grieved for healing to occur. The loss doesn't disappear, but the grief can, and our experience of the loss can shift. In order to release and reclaim our stuck energy, we need to let go of being a victim, regardless of how long we have been holding on, and fully explore and express the grief. In doing so, we open the space to become fully present to opportunities that are available to us in our lives.

"Finished, one feels free, relieved, peaceful, energized, even joyous, with the flood of new energy from within. Finished, we are free to remember and to love without pain, sorrow, or regret."

— JUDY TATELBAUM, *The Courage to Grieve*

Moving through Grief to Wholeness

"Grief can be a path to self-realization because in the process of grieving we acknowledge that which we choose not to lose. In the art of losing we can choose who we will be. We break but we break open so that we can include more of life, more of love."

— DEBORAH MORRIS CORYELL, *Good Grief, Healing Through the Shadow of Loss*

Every one of the women who Kani asked to interview for this book was eager to participate in the project and share her experience of *missed motherhood*. At the end of the interviews, most of them spontaneously mentioned that, in talking about it with Kani, they experienced a surprising energetic, emotional shift. One even felt a release of physical tension in her back. This was true even though they had all, in the past, worked by themselves on dealing with the sadness. As a result of Kani's interest and listening, they experienced a non-judgmental, supportive witness to their story.

We need a cultural shift that recognizes the overwhelming percentage of women who have experienced *missed motherhood* and then teaches us—individually, with each other, as a community, as a culture—how to support them.

Yes, a woman who experiences *missed motherhood* needs to know what to do on her own—that is the beginning of her healing. But the rest of us also need to know *how* to acknowledge a woman's loss and honor her healing journey so she is supported in moving from isolation and separation to experiencing her belonging and wholeness. Then all of us who have suffered *missed motherhood* can come out of hiding.

As we learn to process the loss of *missed motherhood*, the skills developed can then be extrapolated to dealing with loss in general. For the more than 20 years that we have been leading eight-day, personal development workshops called the Hoffman Process, as well as being intimately involved with clients as life coaches, we have taught and experienced the practical aspects of grieving loss, healing and coming into wholeness. While there are wonderful books available on grieving, none encompass all that could be effective in specifically healing the grief that occurs as a result of *missed motherhood*, or how, as a society, we can acknowledge and integrate its widespread occurrence as a part of life.

With the varied family and societal histories about how to deal with loss, there are beliefs held by individuals and communities that actually resist effective grieving and healing. Within each of the cultural communities, these are so consistent and unconscious that they can just seem like the truth.

Current research is discovering more and more about how our brains develop and operate. It appears that we are born without an operating system beyond the automatic biological functions. Our brains become *programmed* by modeling what we perceive as we experience life in our specific environment during our early years. This is handy because it means that we can be born into any family, any culture and, without conscious effort, learn how to fit right in. We take on the beliefs, attitudes and moods of our caregivers, our parents. Another aspect of this early programming is that it is lodged in our *implicit* memory system, which functions automatically to anticipate with lightning speed throughout our life what to expect and how to be in situations. As Daniel Siegel, M.D., explains in his book, *The Developing Mind*: "Our lives can become shaped by reactivations of implicit memory, which lack a sense that anything is being recalled. We simply enter these engrained states and experience them as the reality of our present experience."

By the age of two, our brains have begun to develop *explicit* memories, which we can recall, and which give us a sense of time and sequence of events. Now the modeling of our environment is becoming more conscious, but is still happening. As humans, we need to know how to fit in and belong. The ability to recall events that we know were in the past can serve as proof about the way life is, so we feel even more certain. Before we are fully aware of the implications or validity, we are learning our families' formulas for how we need to be or what we need to do to belong, succeed, feel worthy, be safe and be loved.

The programmed beliefs, moods and attitudes that we learn implicitly and explicitly greatly impact the manner in which we deal with loss. Remember those glib comments mentioned earlier? It's as if they come out of nowhere and we hold them as truth, even when the evidence does not support them.

If these beliefs are not the truth, we need to discover what is. This requires curiosity—the willingness to explore, to uncover what's hidden in the depths of our being, to examine what we don't know and discover what we do feel and think. Ignoring or suppressing our feelings sends them underground, only to resurface again; it does not resolve them. Exploring, discovering and expressing feelings and thoughts does allow grieving to occur and movement toward wholeness to happen. Being heard, acknowledged and validated by others supports and encourages integration and belonging in the community.

Healing happens in three arenas if we only know what to do and have an understanding and space to do it in. This is the focus of the next chapters of this book. In each of these arenas, specific exercises and activities are proposed and described. They include what we can do for ourselves as well as how we can help others effectively support us.

First, there is the work that a woman can do by herself. For most women, this has been the only arena that has been available. And, often, even this knowledge has been elusive.

The second arena is with others in our lives—our spouse or partner, family and friends. Many of us have attempted this and been disappointed with the results, since neither we nor they knew how to proceed. We hear phrases that are meant to be helpful and supportive, but often leave little room to express our feelings and be acknowledged.

The third arena is in our communities. For the most part, this is uncharted territory. There are funerals if someone dies and, in some communities, there are rituals recognizing stillbirths or miscarriages. But with the great number of women experiencing one or more episodes of *missed motherhood*, there is the potential for raising awareness and incorporating expanded ways to acknowledge loss, honor grieving and support life.

"Not knowing how to handle the pain of grief, we avoid it, not realizing it is the pain of loss we are trying to avoid. ...Yet by avoiding grief we turn our backs to the help that grief offers, thus prolonging the pain."
— ELIZABETH KUBLER-ROSS,
On Grief and Grieving

Healing Activities Accomplished Alone

"Healing is embracing what is most feared; healing is opening what has been closed, softening what has hardened into obstruction, healing is learning to trust life."
— JEANNE ACHTERBERG

Depending on our learned patterns, there are unhealthy ways that we may find ourselves using when we are trying to deal with feelings. The following are just a few examples.

- We minimize or dismiss feelings: *It's not so bad, I can get pregnant again. It was my choice so I don't have the right to feel sad. Don't wallow; get on with your life. It was God's will.*

- We indulge in and hang onto suffering: *I'll never get over this. My life is ruined. Life is unfair and I'm a victim. Without a child, life isn't worth living.*

- We hide our feelings from others: *If you have nothing good to say, keep quiet. Don't bother others. You should be ashamed of yourself; hide. Don't air your dirty laundry in public.*

- We judge and blame ourselves or others to make sense of suffering and loss: *I'm flawed and don't belong. It's selfish not to have children. I don't fit in. Don't go where you don't belong.*

- We deny, repress and disconnect from feelings: *Forget about it. Keep busy so you don't think about it or feel it. Time heals all wounds. Rise above it.*

Research has shown that it is powerful to explore, discover and appropriately express feelings using language. In his book, *Opening Up, The Healing Power of Expressing Emotions*, James Pennebaker, Ph.D., reports that inhibiting expression can place people at risk for major diseases and that confronting and expressing our deepest feelings and thoughts can boost the immune system and have short-term and long-term health benefits. Over the last 25 years, we have regularly witnessed this happening with our students in the Hoffman Process, which includes focused verbal, physical and written experiences of expressing feelings and thoughts.

Expression is a proven path to healing, freedom and wholeness. The first step necessary is exploration, especially of the feelings and thoughts that we have hidden, repressed, minimized or denied. Without the exploration and subsequent discovery, we can express the easily accessible feelings, such as sadness and crying endlessly, but never get down to the core issues and move beyond the past into the present. If we are willing to delve deeply into the feelings and identify what they all are—and then discover and express the false belief systems that hold the feelings in place—we can begin to move toward healing. Putting our feelings and thoughts into words, written or spoken, moves us toward healing.

Our expectations about life and our sense of self are often seriously impacted by *missed motherhood*. Children or no children is a huge part of our definition of how we want our life to unfold—it's really a centerpiece, which we envision being able to control.

Women who choose to be childfree also benefit from acknowledgment of and support for their decision, and the gains and losses that are incurred. For now, they still live outside the mainstream, what is considered the norm. Since they chose to be childfree, acknowledging what they have lost out on can be perceived as regret, even when that is not the case. Each of us wants to feel that we belong, that we are part of the whole.

EXPLORATION, DISCOVERY & EXPRESSION THROUGH WRITING

"The simple act of putting down your deepest thoughts and feelings on paper is one of the most powerful and effective means to ease and ultimately heal sorrow."
— SUSAN ZIMMERMAN,
Writing to Heal the Soul

Extensive research shows that writing is an excellent tool. You can do it by yourself, without worrying about what anyone else will think or feel or judge. You can do it over time, going deeper and wider as you expand the access to your inner world. Sometimes we get stuck in sadness, hurt or anger, or we try to limit or avoid those feelings; we then remain unaware of what is underneath, driving our feelings and keeping them in place. As you continue to write, you can move through the stuck places.

Following are some exercises to help explore, discover and express the feelings and the thoughts that accompany them. Depending on the extent and details of your loss, select the ones that challenge you—choose the ones that you *don't* want to do. It's often the case that the more we want to avoid looking, the more we need the exploration. There is no right sequence. There is no necessity to do them all. Listen to your inner guidance.

Acknowledge, Validate and Claim the Loss

Write your story of loss without minimizing it. Go back to the beginning, when you just had your dream. Describe in detail what happened to create the loss and the pain you felt then and are feeling now. Keep exploring how you felt at each step, what your thoughts were, how your body felt, what choices you had, what decisions you made, how you feel about your decisions. Pull the feelings and thoughts, all the details, out of storage in the closet of your mind and heart and put them into words on paper. As you remember, notice and record what you are now feeling and thinking and then write about it. Include positive as well as negative feelings and thoughts. You are the only one who is going to read this, so take off all the limits.

There is healing power in telling your story. Go for it! It can be effective to write for 20 to 30 minutes a day for a number of days. While you are writing, and when you just finish writing, you might feel sadness and grief more deeply. Over time, through the expression of your feelings and thoughts in words, the energy stuck in grief should release. You may then experience more space within and gain a wider perspective of the loss as a part of the journey of your life.

Identify the Beliefs You Hold that Impact Your Situation

Our belief systems make meaning out of our lives—what we think and feel about ourselves, what others think and feel about us, what we think and feel about others. What are your beliefs about having children, not having children, having a miscarriage or abortion, giving a child up for adoption, being unable to become pregnant, running out of time to have children, being ambivalent, or choosing to be childfree? What do those beliefs tell you about yourself as a result of your experiences of *missed motherhood*—about your worth, lovability, success, safety, belonging? Make a list.

Once the lists are made, look around you, examine the basis for the beliefs and the expectation they have created for you. Take a look at how they are limiting your experience of life. Often what we believe and what we experience contradict each other. Recognition of the contradictions allows us to reevaluate these beliefs and move through the maze to a new future. For Kani, once it became clear that her life was not over, even though her original dream was impossible, she was able to create a path to move forward productively and with enthusiasm.

Create and Explore a Dialogue Within

Consider yourself as being comprised of four aspects: intellect, emotions, body and spirit. From this place, you can create dialogues between these different aspects and discover all sorts of things about yourself and the issue of *missed motherhood*. For example, your intellect could dialogue with your emotions, expressing curiosity, asking questions, receiving information and validating feelings. Your emotions and intellect could ask for what is needed for greater awareness and presence of each aspect. Your body is often the container for repressed emotions and, if accessed, is a rich source of information. You can call forth your spirit or essence—the source of intuition, creativity and inner wisdom—to help you deal with the challenges. Listen with curiosity. Listening to all aspects allows you to discover what is going on inside of you.

For example, check in with each aspect and make notes. Have your emotional self name and describe the feelings you have about *missed motherhood*. Have your intellect name and describe the thoughts and beliefs about your situation. Have your body describe the sensations you experience. What has your essence or spirit intuited about your situation and what does she offer you as guidance? Ask each aspect what it wants to say to any other aspect. For example, your emotions might ask the spirit for support, or ask the intellect to listen. In doing this, you learn more about the complexity of who you are and what you need to feel whole.

Vision for Your Life: Past and Future

We each hold conscious and unconscious ideas about how our lives will unfold. In this exercise, you are going to look at what your vision *has* been and where you have arrived at this point in your life. Then you will create a vision for how you will move forward. In consciously creating a vision, we have the opportunity to reflect on not just the outcome, but how we want to explore and navigate our lives.

Step 1: Write a Description of the Vision You had for Your Life
Describe what you expected and hoped for. Include relationships with a partner as well as family, how you felt about having or not having children, where you would live and your living environment, work you would do, how you would spend your days, and your place in the community. This writing can be done over a number of days. Keep adding to it until you have included all the dimensions that you have held as important for your life. Very importantly, name what you expected to feel in each of the areas of your life. In writing about it, you can bring it all into the open and discover all the dimensions of the vision you have been holding as necessary for you to have a full and happy life. Once you have accomplished writing this, you are ready for the next step.

Step 2: Exploring Your Vision
• Make a list of the parts of the vision you have described that you now have in your life. In looking at this list, note how you expected to feel when you had achieved each aspect and how you feel now that you are actually experiencing that aspect of your vision. Is there any discrepancy between how you expected to feel and how you actually feel?

• Then make a list of the parts of your original vision that are currently missing. Notice how you feel about their absence as well as how you expected to feel if you did have them.

Step 3: Create a New, Revised Vision—Reflecting on Your Life
Describe everything that is important to you now, including how you deal with the unexpected challenges in life.

CREATE A RITUAL

"Rituals keep us centered in the present, and at the same time allow us to deal with the past and envision our futures in a healthy way."
— Barbara Bizious,
The Joys of Everyday Rituals

A ritual is action taken to acknowledge a transition or change—an ending or beginning—and can be a pathway to connection and wholeness within ourselves. Intuitively, women have created and experienced rituals to deal with the loss of an unborn child or infertility. Five of the women in this book (Carol, Bella, Sophia, Alexa and Barbara) describe rituals they experienced alone or with others.

Some women create or receive a name for each unborn child, others do not. (In doing the ritual, you may find that names come to you.) Women who were never able to become pregnant, or who choose to be childfree, can acknowledge the children that never were. A ritual may be something done once, with no permanent record, or it might involve writing that is saved in a special place or burned in a ceremony. Your ritual might involve an object or plants that become a part of your life, or it might be something you do regularly at a special time. You might combine elements of some or all of the following ideas. Allow your intuition and creativity to guide you.

Dialogue with the Spirit of the Unborn Child or Children

This was such a powerful experience for Kani almost 20 years after one of her experiences with *missed motherhood* that we introduced it into the Hoffman Process. During this ritual, we offer a flower to every woman and man who has ever lost a pregnancy; if there have been multiple losses, we offer a flower for each loss. We suggest they find a lovely spot in nature, place the flower there, and then speak with the spirit of that little being, saying all there is to say. Then we suggest that the student ask for and listen to a message from that little being. This often surprises the students and frequently brings tears to their eyes, even when they thought they had already moved on and put it behind them. Many students are awed by what it brings up in them, even long after the event, and the healing that ensues.

Write a Letter to the Child or Children

As in the dialogue above, share your feelings and thoughts with the unborn children in writing. Write down what you have learned about yourself and what you may have missed. Say whatever it is you have to say. The letter may be brief or it may be extensive, especially if you have suffered a number of pregnancy losses or were never able to become pregnant. This can be an opportunity to acknowledge your choices and mourn your losses. You can go to a quiet, special place and read the letter out loud, alone or with one other person as a loving, silent witness. If you choose, you may bury the letter or burn it.

Honoring Loss with Objects or Plants

One woman created a special section of her garden to honor her lost children; another planted a flowering tree whose presence is a beautiful reminder; another made clay figures, wrapped them in silk and buried them close together in her garden. Statues of various sizes have been placed inside the home and outside in the garden as memorials. There are also numerous websites that sell jewelry to commemorate the loss.

"It's not forgetting that heals. It's remembering."

—Amy Greene, *Bloodroot*

Healing Through Sharing With Others

"Too often we underestimate the power of a touch, a smile, a kind word, a listening ear, an honest compliment, or the smallest act of caring, all of which have the potential to turn a life around."

—LEO BUSCAGLIA

As women who have experienced loss and grief, the two of us (Kani and Barbara) know what power there is in sharing—in putting feelings and thoughts into words, expressing them out loud, being listened to and heard by another, validating what is. We are no longer alone. The experience is now seen and acknowledged by others. Expression is powerful in accomplishing movement and achieving healing. The goal is integrating the experience of loss into one's life.

The challenge in sharing is recognizing what we are looking for from the person we are sharing with and selecting appropriate people. We can't assume that others will know what will be supportive of our healing. Often, people feel a responsibility to solve our problems for us and the power of just listening goes unrecognized. Yet, we can guide them in what will be supportive of us. In fact, it is our responsibility to be explicit in what we need—to let the listener know.

In revealing our loss, we don't need to be fixed. We need to be heard. Each of the women who revealed her story in this book found healing in taking the space and time to explore and discover her own feelings and thoughts and speak them out loud. For many of them, it was the first time they had shared and were listened to with respect, curiosity and without judgment.

SOME SUGGESTED GUIDELINES FOR SHARING

Take the Initiative to Set Up a Time and Environment

Let the person know you want to share with them and just want to be listened to. Ask them, "Is this a good time or what would be a good time?" Recognize that the other person may be in a place in their life where they can't be available to you in the way you need. Respect their choice.

Consider where you want to be—perhaps in your home? At a restaurant? Walking in nature? Then consider the physical orientation between you and your listener: Would you like to be facing the person? Sitting or standing or walking next to them? Sitting on the floor? You can also share on the telephone if you prefer. In any case, really think about what will be best for you in your setting of choice and make that clear to the person. When you are speaking, do you want them to keep a neutral face? Would you like them to make sounds to affirm they are listening or do you want them to be absolutely silent? Let the listener know what will support you.

With some people in your life, sharing through writing—a letter, an email, a blog—may be the best choice. When you are writing, you are in complete control of the message, without any possibility of interruption. You also have the opportunity to edit the message before sending it. In doing this, it is helpful to let the recipient know what you want from them, what will support you. Often, what is wanted and needed is just to be heard and validated.

Know What You Want to Share
Your sharing with another grows out of what you have shared with yourself as a result of the previous chapter. Acknowledge, validate and claim the loss without minimizing it. Express what happened to create the loss and pain you were feeling then, and are feeling now. Share what you felt, what your thoughts were, how your body felt, what choices you had, what decisions you made. And share the beliefs you have held that have impacted your situation. Share what you have learned about yourself. Include positive as well as negative feelings and thoughts.

Ask for What You Need or Want
When you approach the person you'd like to share with, consider saying: "What I'd like to talk with you about is an important time in my life that I haven't shared before. I wonder if you would be wiling to listen in silence, with patience and curiosity, letting any assumptions go?"

If the person is agreeable, you can also offer guidelines to help them respond to you: "After I have said what I have to say, you may have questions that you think could help me tell my story more fully. You could ask me things like: 'Besides sharing with me, have you found other ways to process the experience?' 'What would real support look like for you?' 'What would you have liked to have happened at the time that didn't happen?' 'What effect did the experience have on your life then and what effect does it have now?'"

Acknowledge the Feelings that Arise in the Process of Sharing

While you are sharing, and when you just finish sharing, you might feel sadness and grief more deeply. You might feel calm and peace. The verbal expression of your feelings and thoughts, like the written expression, releases energy stuck in grief. You then can experience more space within and gain a wider perspective of the loss as a part of the journey of your life.

As the Listener, Relax into Listening with a Curious Mind

"The most basic and powerful way to connect to another person is to listen. Just listen. Perhaps the most important thing we ever give each other is our attention ... A loving silence often has far more power to heal and to connect than the most well-intentioned words."

—RACHEL NAOMI REMEN

The healing for the speaker is in the telling, putting her thoughts and feelings into words and then sharing them with you and being heard. Your silent listening opens a space for this to happen. Even if you have had a similar experience of *missed motherhood*, resist saying "I know just how you feel." We don't actually know how the other person feels or what the experience meant to her and her life. By listening with curiosity, we can find out. By sharing and being heard, the speaker has the opportunity to explore and discover more of what her feelings and thoughts were at the time of the loss and what they are now.

If you are asked to listen, you are not being asked to fix the situation or offer advice. Consider that a separate request for advice from the speaker is necessary before you offer any.

Once the speaker has shared all that she has to say, and if you have a *missed motherhood* experience of your own that you want to share with her, then you can ask if that would be okay. She may or may not be open to it at that time. Honor her choice. Follow the same guidelines in what you share. Resist the impulse to share as a way of offering advice.

Consider Whom You Want to Share with

Is it an individual, a group of close friends, family members, a women's group you belong to or a grief-healing group that you might want to join? Whether individually or in a group, be conscious and be grounded in the guidelines that support you and share them with the listeners.

You may be moved to find other women who have had similar experiences of *missed motherhood* and create a group in which you can all experience sharing, listening and validating each other. You may find it supports your group to read this book and do some of the exercises together.

CREATE A RITUAL

"Ritual is recognizing a life change and doing something to honor and support the change...Engaging in a ritual allows your mind to expand, your mood to change, and your spirits to rise."

— BARBARA BIZIOUS,
The Joys of Everyday Rituals

As with group sharing, you have control over how simple or elaborate the ritual is, what is included, who the active participants are, who is invited and how people are included in the activity. Carol did it with family, Bella included family and friends in a memorial service, a friend initiated and led the ritual for Barbara, and Alexa created a simple act in the presence of a friend to finalize a decision. In addition, Sophia invited the creation of a group blessing in preparation for moving on.

Guidelines for Creating a Ritual with Others

"The purpose of ritual is to increase balance and connection within ourselves, with each other, with the world, and with the subtle but powerful rhythms and energies of the cosmos and the spiritual realm."

— RENEE BECK & SYDNEY BARBARA METRICK,
The Art of Ritual

Define the Purpose of the Ritual
• Honoring your *missed motherhood* experience
• Acknowledging buried loss; naming and honoring the loss
• Recognition of your choices
• Celebration of the life you have created

Consider Collaborating in Creating the Ritual Structure
This could be with a friend, a coach, a minister; or use one of the books in the resource section.

Create the Structure, Location and Logistics of the Ritual
Decide who will lead the ritual, you or another, and clarify what you want to do and where you want to do it. The ritual may include you reading a letter to the child that wasn't born, sharing your vision for

the future and memorial activities like planting a tree, tossing stones into water and other suggestions from the previous chapter.

Identify Who You Want to have Participate and What You Want Them to Do

This may be people who might provide music, sing, read poems, write something, read something, light a candle. There might be an activity they do alone or that you all do together.

ATTEND A FACILITATED GROUP HEALING OR WORKSHOP

In working with this material, it's likely that you will discover old beliefs that have limited your life and kept you in denial or stuck in grief. The recognition of unresolved feelings and thoughts can be a great opportunity for transformation and moving forward in your life. A facilitated workshop is supportive at a time like this.

"Women, Children, Choice & Loss, Honoring Our Wholeness"— A Workshop

From years of working with people in intense personal growth and healing environments, we created this workshop for women of all ages with unresolved issues around *missed motherhood*. The workshop brings awareness and healing in a safe, supportive space where you can explore and acknowledge the impact *missed motherhood* has had on your life. You are invited to express and honor your feelings, participate in healing rituals and witness for each other. Visit the website at www.missedmotherhood.com

The Hoffman Process

An eight-day, intensive residential course of personal discovery and development which allows you to examine your life, your losses and your behavior and empowers you to make lasting changes. You can read about it in the book, *Journey into Love, Ten Steps to Wholeness*, (see book list) and visit the website: www.hoffmaninstitute.org.

Look for Workshops Dealing with Grief and Loss in Your Area or on the Internet.

"Whenever unfinished feelings are perceived, even years later, it is time to finish. It is never too late to complete our grief."

— JUDY TATELBAUM, *The Courage to Grieve*

Initiating Community Recognition and Inclusion

A Vision for the Future

"In a futile attempt to erase our past, we deprive the community of our healing gift. If we conceal our wounds out of fear and shame, our inner darkness can neither be illuminated nor become a light for others."
—Brennan Manning,
Abba's Child

We support a vision where *missed motherhood* is recognized, validated and honored as a part of community life. As we can see from the stories in this book, what's missing in many women's lives is a general recognition and place for *missed motherhood*. There is Mother's Day, Father's Day, Veterans Day, wedding and birth announcements. Except for funerals, we rarely recognize suffering, pain, loss or absence. Loss is considered private, perhaps even shameful, as it can be around pregnancy loss, infertility or childlessness.

Missed motherhood occurs in the lives of as many as 75% of women. Recent research suggests that an event can become a trauma in the brain depending on how the affected person is received and held in the community. Acknowledgment of the prevalence and impact of *missed motherhood* needs to be integrated into the community so that all women can experience inclusion and wholeness. Our vision includes services, rituals and gatherings that recognize and support the healing of *missed motherhood*.

"We can't undo bad things that happen. But maybe we can reshape the environment that exists in their wake."

— David Dobbs, *A New Focus on the 'Post' in Post-Traumatic Stress,*
New York Times, December 24, 2012

COMMUNITY EVENTS

"We don't heal in isolation, but in community."
— S. KELLEY HARRELL, *Gift of the
Dreamtime—Reader's Companion*

Gatherings Honoring Missed Motherhood:
Celebration of Belonging

As a result of the work we have done and the need we have clarified, we have created a community gathering to honor women who have experienced any of our categories of *missed motherhood*, including women who are childless by choice or circumstance. The gathering provides a supportive environment for a woman to bring more of herself into connection with community, to be seen and to be honored. It also offers the community an opportunity to recognize and honor the broad spectrum of the experience of the feminine. The gatherings include sharing, meditations, ritual and music. For more information, visit www.missedmotherhood.com.

Mother's Day Service: *Honoring the Feminine*

Mother's Day can be a painful time for women who have experienced pregnancy loss, infertility or childlessness. In 2003, as a result of the work she was doing with her sister, Barbara, and other women, Kani initiated the idea of a Mother's Day service that honors all women, not just mothers. She and her Unity minister co-created and led a service they called "Honoring the Feminine." The following year, an alternate version, featuring the "Generations of Women," was created. Both versions of this service are included in the Resources section.

Other Community Ceremonies

Since we started exploring *missed motherhood* over a decade ago, we have been able to find a few community experiences that acknowledge pregnancy loss, but none that include infertility or the choice not to have children. These few examples are a beginning; however, they do not include all of our five categories of *missed motherhood*:

Our Spirit Babies Ceremony in San Francisco, California

This interfaith service was created to honor babies lost through abortion, miscarriage and stillbirth. People are invited to come together in a sacred space to honor themselves, their lost babies and one another. The ceremony has taken place during the Winter

Solstice, when the darkest time of year welcomes the beginning of the next season's growing light. This service was created by a circle of people whose lives were touched by pregnancy loss. For more information go to spiritbabies.org.

Saying Goodbye Services in the United Kingdom

A couple in the U.K. conceived of the "Saying Goodbye" memorial services to honor babies lost in pregnancy or infancy. The services are organized by the couple, (who have lost five babies through miscarriage and now have two young children) through their events company in partnership with a number of other U.K. miscarriage associations. Scheduled to be held in 20 churches across the United Kingdom, the hope is that these services will bring some peace to the participants, regardless of their religious or spiritual belief systems. The services follow an Anglican format and include secular music, poetry and other elements. Visit www. sayinggoodbye.org to learn more.

Search on the Internet

It is possible to find numerous examples of rabbis, synagogues and other spiritual leaders and organizations that are creating and modifying rituals and services to honor pregnancy loss.

We encourage women to reach out in their communities, to initiate new and creative ways to support, embrace and honor all women's experiences and to encourage an environment of inclusion and belonging. We invite you to introduce the Mother's Day Service to your neighborhood or group and to let it inspire original ceremonies and motivate your community to create services that celebrate and honor all women for their creativity and contributions.

Moving Forward

"There are times when life sharpens, things come into focus and, gradually, you become aware that you are standing before a threshold. There is no way back to where you were before, and there is no way out but through."
— John O'Donohue

As women who have experienced *missed motherhood*, we have the opportunity to heal ourselves and support and honor the healing of others. By stepping out of the shadows of *missed motherhood* by revealing ourselves and sharing our feelings and thoughts appropriately, we can move ourselves and our communities toward integration and wholeness. We can claim belonging, not as an exception, but rather as part of the diversity of experience that comprises the whole. This is a gift to all women. It is a gift to our communities and our culture. It is time to break the silence, open the doors on what has been unexpressed and claim our belonging. We are not alone.

Missed motherhood is something that happens in the context of a woman's life, often in multiple ways. The experience is not limited to the specific events; instead, it encompasses the impact *missed motherhood* has over the course of her life—the way pregnancy, childbearing and absence of children are held and integrated by the woman herself, by the people around her and by the culture. Loss and confusion are common. Women have a tendency to "buck up" and handle challenges without asking for support, such as getting pregnant when they can't imagine have a child, having a miscarriage or abortion, trying to conceive month after month with no results, enduring procedures that consume years of their lives, considering whether or not to have children, realizing it's too late. Often, they just deal with these traumas on their own: *I'm strong. I can figure it out.*

As life coaches and teachers, we—Barbara and Kani—have witnessed women stumbling upon the unintegrated experience of *missed motherhood*, the unexpected shudder, tears, anger and grief. We find meticulous memories of joy and loss tucked away in rarely visited corners. We find women are grateful for acknowledgment and healing rituals. We are struck that women frequently do not share with their daughters their own experiences of *missed motherhood,* or their ambivalent path towards becoming a parent, so the knowledge is not passed on in this fundamental area of a woman's life. And then, each subsequent generation invents itself according to assumptions and beliefs and nonverbal cues.

Each woman's experience needs to be held with respect and reverence. There are often feelings of shame and failure around loss that is hidden. We need to open the space for each woman to come out of the closet, be seen as she is, respected and honored as whole, whatever her losses and choices. Let there be light! The more opportunity there is for a woman to stand up, state what has happened in her life and be recognized that she belongs—whether with herself, with another, in groups, gatherings or services—the more our culture can embrace the full range of experience. Any movement in this direction is valuable.

"It is only when we have the courage to face things exactly as they are, without any self-deception or illusion, that a light will develop out of events by which the path to success may be recognized."

— I CHING HEXAGRAM 5

Some Resources

Mother's Day Service: "Honoring the Feminine"

©2003, revised 2012 Rev. Sherry Lady and Kani Comstock

Order of Service

PRAYER OF DEDICATION

We welcome everyone to this service on Mother's Day—a special day of honoring our mothers and honoring the feminine and the contribution of the feminine energy in the world. We dedicate this service to that energy and to all of life. Let's close our eyes.

Allow yourself to become fully present to this moment, present and available to the living, loving spirit of the feminine as we dedicate our time together. We give thanks, Great Spirit, that in your infinite creative wisdom you understood the need for balance in our lives. You brought us forth from both the feminine and masculine energy so in partnership we could together create life in the fullest on this planet. As we honor that creation today, we call forth from each heart the coming together into the oneness and the fullness of all that is. We dedicate this service to the beauty, joy and harmony that is possible. We dedicate this service to the spirit of the living, loving god that dwells in each person on the planet. We dedicate this service to every person who has come here to share in this day. We give thanks for this allness in the oneness. And so it is. Amen.

HONORING THE FEMININE

Select a woman to represent each of the following qualities. Call each woman forth one-by-one to light a candle as you recognize their contribution. After lighting a candle, have them stand with you until all women are represented.

Givers of Physical Life

Thank you for agreeing to become a vessel to bring forth new life on this earth. Thank you for caring for children lovingly, providing a spiritual base, recognizing and nurturing their unique being and individual path, accepting the lifetime commitment of love and care and recognizing that your children will always be a part of your life. We honor you.

Caregivers and Nurturers

As mother, teacher, nurse, counselor, minister, you care for the health and well-being of others from the goodness and generosity of your heart. You nurture their growth, their connection to spirit. You support their learning in daily life and during times of challenge. You have chosen this path of contribution. We honor you.

Pursuers of Knowledge and Intelligence

With a marvelous willingness to ask questions, you boldly seek information, search out answers, open yourself to new perspectives and greater knowledge. You don't hold back. You go ahead and explore uncharted territory, challenge current wisdom and create new understandings that open the world for the rest of us. We honor you.

Earth Mothers, Gardeners & Soil Caretakers

Honoring the earth that brings forth the abundance and beauty of life around us—the flowers, trees, fruits and veggies—is core to your nature. You understand the gift that the earth is and recognize all it brings to our life. You treasure it, watch over it and remind us of its sacredness. We honor you.

Protectors of the Waters

Water is life-giving, life-producing, nurturing and cleansing. With bodies composed of 90% water, from our earliest moments each of us was nurtured by and in the waters of the womb. The oceans, lakes, rivers and streams cover most of the surface of our world. You recognize water as a force of nature that supports us and supports life. We honor you.

Visionaries

You look forward, perceive opportunities, recognize the vastness and limitlessness of the skies, the magnificence of the sun and the moon and the stars. You perceive the invisible as real, bring forth fresh insight like a cool breeze that expands our world. We honor you.

Wise Wild Women

With many years of experience, challenges and triumphs, you have the courage to trust the voice within and act from this inner wisdom. You listen and perceive, receive others as they are. You speak truth, act from your heart and let your soul be seen. You dance with exuberance and live to the fullest. We honor you.

MEDITATION

Let's begin our time of meditation together by closing our eyes and feeling centered and grounded as we breathe. Feel your breath bringing the Light into your being. With every breath we bring in Light and we breathe out any heaviness, distraction or darkness. So with every breath we take, we increase and expand the Light within us that touches our own Light. Feel that expansion and that blessing within...

Today is a time of honoring your own unique contribution to life, of honoring and celebrating your belonging, of honoring your place in the whole amazing mystery of life. Experience the Light abundant within you and around you and around all of us here today. Light that is you, that is me and that connects each of us to all the wonderful beings here together this morning. Breathe in and experience the vibrancy of the Light...

And as you breathe, look at the challenges you have faced, the choices you have made in life, the path you have traveled as an individual, as a unique being in this life... Allow yourself to see these choices, this path, with a sense of gratitude for what has been and where you have come to in life, all the gifts that you have been given, the skills you have received and honed and honored as yours, and your way of contributing in life...

And as you breathe, look at the major choices you made in your life, the choices that really determined the path that you are on, your path of contribution. Remember the challenges you faced where the path you had to choose was uncertain and perhaps difficult. Acknowledge the learning that came as a result of those challenging choices—and the learning that came in facing the challenge and moving forward.

As you name those challenges and those learnings for yourself, honor yourself for each step taken. Some you handled better than others perhaps, but honor yourself for walking your path, for making choices where choices were available, for being who you are in this life, for growing, listening to that wise voice within you that leads you from Spirit, from that Light within.

Look at how you've been able to handle things that came your way that wouldn't have been your choices. Know that how you handled them was your choice. And as you trace your step on this path that you're on, that you have traveled, this path you are traveling now, acknowledge the Spirit that has always been with you, that has helped you move along this path, that has helped you explore your path and expand with it, that has enabled you to look forward with vision.

It is time now to forgive yourself for any actions or choices that you may have made that you wish you hadn't, but that was the best you could do at the time. As you breathe in, feel your breath filling you with light, nurturing you and bathing you with light. In that bathing and nurturing Light, experience your forgiveness. You did the best you could at that time... Breathe out and release any remaining pain, sorrow, grief or regret. As you continue to breathe, acknowledge that it was all on your path, it was all part of the journey of your life. At each step you took, you were guided. Bless all those in your life who nurtured you and walked with you on your path.

Know that you belong and you are whole and you are here and you are blessed. Know that you are a contribution to those in your life. Feel the blessing of the Light throughout your being filling you, nurturing you and let it be so. Sit in the silence of the blessing and allow the music to support you.

For all you are and all you are yet to be, we give thanks. Amen.

MOTHER'S DAY MESSAGE

Every time a child is born, there is an opportunity to teach that child a sense of well-being, a feeling of worth, a belief in their ability to accomplish great things in their lives. Each person the child comes in contact with during their growing-up years has the opportunity to influence the child's perception of his or her own innate value and worth. This includes parents, teachers, spiritual leaders, neighbors, childcare providers and community members.

One of the most accurate statements ever made about the raising of children was that, "It takes a village to raise a child." For children raised in remote areas, the family, along with some neighbors, is the "village." The size of the village increases for children who grow up in more populated areas. In these larger areas, the variety of influence expands. Each of these people has the opportunity to make a difference in the life of a child and, through that connection, an opportunity to be part of the enhancement of society.

This is Mother's Day and we honor those women who provided the nurturing, physical, intra-uterine environment in which we each began our journey toward taking our place in the world. Mothers are incredible gifts to us all and, since we each had one, they are a blessed necessity. We honor the women who brought us into life and mothered us. We honor the women here who have brought forth life and nurtured their children.

Along with mothers, there are wonderful, creative, nurturing women and men who, either by choice or circumstance, did not become parents, yet they took the opportunity to be with children in some of the capacities I have mentioned. Their support and guidance can add incredibly to the parenting of children. For those in our childhood and in our children's childhoods, we feel gratitude.

It is so important for a child—and we were all children at one time—to have a supportive community of people who assist, nurture, care for, pray for, teach and entertain. There is an old saying: "The hand that rocks the cradle rules the world." I prefer to say: "The hands that rock the cradle can change the world, making it a better place for all."

We all belong to a community village and on this day are choosing to honor not only mothers, but all who play an important role in the life of that community and its children.

I ask all women to stand,

READING: *(read by a woman)*

"Be a Queen"
by Oprah Winfrey at the Spelman College Commencement in 1993.
Text can be found at http://christinaville.wordpress.com/be-a-queen/

READER:
"Look at us! We are all Queens!
Let us own our power and our glory!"

MINISTER: Feel your power and glory as you sit down.

BELONGING: INDIVIDUAL VOICES
*(Pre-selected women and men from the congregation stand,
one-by-one, speak their statement, then sit down.)*

I am a creative being and I belong.

I am spirit embodied and I belong.

I am supported by the universe and I belong.

I am seen and accepted for who I am as I am and I belong.

I am filled with Light and I belong.

I am supported and nurtured by this community and I belong.

I nurture others and I belong.

I am love and I belong.

We are all one in spirit and we belong.

BELONGING: COMMUNITY

MINISTER: Everyone stand and read from the insert in your bulletin.

EVERYONE: *name of your church* is a spiritual community where I am accepted for who I am as I am with love and caring. I celebrate my belonging.

MINISTER: We stand for peace in the presence of conflict; for love in the presence of hatred and for forgiveness in the presence of injury. We honor the many names of God, the many paths to God, the many ways to worship God; for there is only one power and presence of God and that God loves each of us equally.

EVERYONE: This is my spiritual community in which I participate. Knowing we are all one in spirit, I celebrate my belonging to this community of spiritual beings. I, *my name*, belong in *name of your church*.

MINISTER: Take this into your heart as you sit down. Now I ask all men to stand.

HONORING THE MASCULINE

MINISTER: God created both women and men as part of the whole. We honor your presence and your contributions to the lives of women, for bringing children into this world and for your support and nurturance of women and children and family and community. Regardless of your lifestyles or how you choose to express who you are, the energy you bring to the planet is balancing energy. Each of us has both female and male energy in us. Stand tall and proud in your maleness and in your feminine. Like *yin* and *yang*, your wholeness supports and encourages the wholeness of us all. Bless you. You may sit down.

Honoring Your Mother

Minister: Close your eyes and bring forth an image of your own mother, the woman who brought you into this world and loved you. Feel your gratitude for all she did for you, for the ways in which she nurtured you, for the many things she taught you, for the ways in which she encouraged you to be your best. Hold her in your heart and give her love. *(pause for silence)*

In closing, we give thanks for the mother energy that nurtures and supports and guides and cares for life.

Special Music – Offering – Community Circle:
Prayer of Protection & Peace Song

Generations of Women
(Alternative to Honoring the Feminine)

Select a girl/woman to represent each of the generations. Call each girl/woman forth one-by-one to light a candle as you recognize their generation. After lighting a candle, have them stand with you until all generations are represented.

0-10 Years Thank you for your willingness to be on the earth at this time and this age. You represent innocence, hope, pure intent and excitement about life. Those of us who are older have much to learn from you about being in the moment, curiosity and adventure. We are touched by your beauty, your joy in even the smallest things, your smile and radiance. You bring forth our joy and we thank you.

11-19 Years You are emerging from childhood into your teen years, such a challenging time of life. These years are a time of transition from being a child to becoming an adult, and new experiences that can bring forth daring, awkwardness, exuberance and exhilaration. As you blossom forth, we begin to see the woman you will become. We support your exploration and growth and wish you a smooth and joyous journey.

20's & 30's You are taking on adulthood and independence and life looms large as you begin to try on your dreams and follow through on commitments. You are making choices and taking action that will define your life's path, and may involve motherhood. There are so many options and opportunities and each step you take adds to your experience of who you are. We are here to support you even as you move further into your own life.

40's & 50's Time has moved swiftly and your family is changing. You may find yourself evaluating what you have already done, looking at what still fits and what no longer fits, what else you want to do, who you really are, separating out what you are still willing to do and what you are no longer willing to do. It is often a time of transition. You can delight in all that you have already done in your life.

60's This is a time to enjoy all that you have created, the many things you have brought forth, the many ways you have contributed to your world and how you do belong. It is also a time to commit to fulfilling your dreams and visions. It's no longer "someday," but rather "if not now, when?" You may begin to experience the emergence of the wise, wild woman who knows her passions and follows them.

70's & 80's Time is more abundant for relationships and connection with yourself and others. You cannot believe how many years have passed and how much you have experienced and how much you have to share. You see life in a broader scope as you lose family and friends while, at the same time, welcoming new life. Freed from the "must-dos," creativity can gush forth in new and different ways and we can treasure the flow.

90's We have given so much and nurtured so many and this is a time of receiving, of being nurtured and cared for by ourselves and others. We can honor our journey and celebrate life. The details of life are not important. May you enjoy the moment and the people and the love and the beingness, treasuring each moment and all that it encompasses.

The text for these services can also be found at:
www.content.unity.org/association/networking/infoXchange/
MothersDayService.pdf

BOOKS

Loss, Choice & Grieving

Women's Bodies, Women's Wisdom, Creating Physical and Emotional Health and Healing. Christiane Northrup M.D. Bantam, 1998, 1994.

The chapter entitled "Our Fertility" includes sections on healing pregnancy loss (abortion and miscarriage), transforming infertility, adoption and fertility as a metaphor. The author discusses the importance of grieving loss and includes some suggestions.

A Woman's Book of Life, The Biology, Psychology, and Spirituality of the Feminine Life Cycle. Joan Borysenko Ph.D. Riverhead Books, 1996.

This book describes the stages of a woman's life. In the section called "Ages 21-28: A Home of One's Own: The Psychobiology of Mating and Motherhood," Borysenko notes that 47% of women in the U.S. have had an abortion by age 45; 2.3 million women seek help for infertility each year; and 7.5 million women (about 13% of women of reproductive age) are infertile or have significant difficulties bearing children. Of all women who have had abortions, 50% felt relief and 50% felt regret or sadness. Borysenko had women talk with the soul of their aborted child.

Born to Live. Gladys Taylor McCarey M.D., foreword by Elisabeth Kubler-Ross. Inkwell, 2001.

Dr. McCarey, an ob/gyn, relates real-life stories of pregnancy and her interpretations, including a spirit-based view of abortion and communication with the unborn. She tells of a woman who spoke with the fetus of an unwanted pregnancy, asked the child to leave and then experienced the miscarriage of that fetus.

The Language of Fertility, A Revolutionary Mind-Body Program for Conscious Conception. Niravi B. Payne and Brenda Lane Richardson, foreword by Christiane Northrup M.D. Harmony, 1997.

This book focuses on eliminating the emotional barriers to the conception and birthing of children. Included is a grief ceremony for mourning the losses of miscarriage, abortion and stillbirth and releasing the unborn child.

Healing Mind, Healthy Woman, Using the Mind-Body
Connection to Manage Stress and Take Control of Your Life.
Alice D. Domar and Henry Dreher. Holt, 1996. Delta, 1997.
This book presents mind-body medicine to reduce stress and increase
wellness in women who are experiencing health challenges including
infertility, multiple miscarriages and low self-esteem. It offers a range
of options to be used alongside conventional medicine for treating
and preventing these conditions. Some of the women resolved their
infertility through adoption or choosing to remain childless.

Good Grief, Healing Through the Shadow of Loss. Deborah Morris
Coryell. The Shiva Foundation, 1997, 1998.
This book discusses loss, grief and healing. It states that our grief
becomes the container for what we feel we have lost and that, in the
process of grieving, we come into some new wholeness. The author
stresses that remembering is an essential ingredient in mourning.

The Girls Who Went Away, The Hidden History of Women Who
Surrendered Children for Adoption in the Decades Before
Roe v. Wade. Ann Fessler. Penquin Books, 2006.
In 2002, Fessler started interviewing women who gave up their children
for adoption between 1945 and 1973, when 1.5 million children were
relinquished to non-family. What is stunning about this book is how
many of these women now, decades later, are still suffering from the loss.

Choice, True Stories of Birth, Contraception, Infertility,
Adoption, Single Parenthood, & Abortion. Karen E. Bener and
Nina deGramont, editors. McAdam/Cage, 2007.
The collected voices of 24 women writers offer a look at the real,
human stories behind the reproductive rights debate, focused on the
meaning of the word "choice."

Childless and Childfree

Childfree After Infertility: Moving from Childlessness to a Joyous
Life. Heather Wardell. iUniverise, Inc., 2003.
Focuses on infertile women and how they have chosen to create happy,
childfree lives. The book's upbeat tone leads the reader, with grace and
humor, through what can be a difficult transition.

Sweet Grapes, How to Stop Being Infertile and Start Living Again.
Jean W. Carter M.D. and Michael Carter. Perspectives Press, revised 1998.
Dr. Jean Carter is an ob/gyn who could not conceive a child. This book offers guidance on how to deal with grief and choose to be childfree. The authors offer a three-step program to move through grief and mourn the loss.

Reconceiving Women, Separating Motherhood from Female Identity. Mardy S. Ireland. Guilford Press, 1993.
Information from 100 women between the ages of 38 and 50 is divided into three categories : childless by choice, childless by delay and childless by infertility or health problems. All of the women are members of the Baby Boom generation.

Two is Enough, A Couple's Guide to Living Childless by Choice.
Laura S. Scott. Seal Press, 2009.
Based on the author's own story and interviews with childless-by-choice couples, this book challenges the notion that parenthood is essential for well-being and happiness.

Complete Without Kids, An Insider's Guide to Childfree Living by Choice or by Chance. Ellen L. Walker Ph.D. Greenleaf Book Group Press, 2011.
This book examines what it means—both the negative and the positive—to be childfree by choice or by circumstance. Offering support, guidance and thought-provoking questions, it is a productive guide for anyone considering the childfree path.

Healing Through Expression

Opening Up, The Healing Power of Expressing Emotions.
James W. Pennebaker Ph.D. The Guilford Press, 1997.
Based on clinical research, this book explains how writing about your losses can improve your health, how long-buried trauma negatively affects your immune system and why it's never too late to heal old emotional wounds.

Writing as a Way of Healing, How Telling our Stories Transforms Our Lives. Louise DeSalvo. Beacon Press, 1999.
Based on 20 years of research, this book shows how a person can use the right kind of writing as a way to heal the emotional and physical wounds of life.

Writing to Heal the Soul, Transforming Grief and Loss Through Writing. Susan Zimmerman. Three Rivers Press, 2002.
This book offers simple yet inspiring writing exercises to help the reader resolve pain as grief is transformed into words of hope and healing.

Journey into Love, Ten Step to Wholeness. Kani Comstock and Marisa Thame. Willow Press, 2000.
This book shows how to identify buried emotions and beliefs that limit natural vitality and expansiveness, how to heal the pain of the past, and offers practical steps to claim one's own authentic power and wholeness, as accomplished in the Hoffman Process.

Rituals

The Joys of Everyday Ritual, Spiritual Recipes to Celebrate Milestones, Ease Transitions, and Make Every Day Sacred. Barbara Biziou. St. Martin's Press, 1999.
In addition to general information about creating a ritual, this book includes rituals for grieving an unborn child.

The Art of Ritual, A guide to Creating and Performing Your Own Ceremonies for Growth and Change. Renée Beck and Sydney Barbara Metrick. Celestial Arts, 1990.
The purpose, relevance, power and need for rituals are discussed, as well as many ritual elements that can be included in a ceremony.

STATISTICS ON MISSED MOTHERHOOD
Available statistics are not delineated into the five categories of *missed motherhood* defined in this book, and many women experience *missed motherhood* in more than one category. Sources for statistics include the National Center for Health Statistics, Center for Disease Control and Prevention, Guttmacher Institute, American Pregnancy Association and www.about.com as well as *A Woman's Book of Life,* cited above.

About the Authors

KANI COMSTOCK was training as a research scientist when she first experienced *missed motherhood.* Her life then took a different course. She has lived and worked in Japan, traveled widely especially in the Pacific region, designed cultural and educational exchange programs, developed and directed four organizations including the Hoffman Institute, and wrote a prior book, *Journey into Love.* For the last few decades, Kani has been a Hoffman Process Teacher and Coach. Throughout life, she has been fascinated with exploring the unknown, striving to understand why we do what we do, and creating programs that enable us to grow into wholeness. She lives in Ashland, Oregon.

BARBARA COMSTOCK studied East Asian cultures, then earned an MS and an MFA in textile art and sculpture. Making art in Nepal, she also assisted on a feature-length documentary filmed at a Buddhist monastery. After years of designing and producing custom-clothing and making and showing her art, she had a life-changing experience and joined the Hoffman Institute. Barbara has delighted in designing and directing programs, teaching in, training teachers for and coaching graduates of the Hoffman Process. It has never been her priority to have children. She lives with her husband, who has been her partner for 25 years, in Ashland, Oregon.